CHRISTIAN PARENTING

CHRISTIAN PARENTING

Raising Children in the Real World

Donna Sinclair and Yvonne Stewart

Westminster/John Knox Press
Louisville, Kentucky

First published in 1990
by Wood Lake Books Inc.
Box 700, Winfield, BC, Canada, V0H 2C0

© 1992 Westminster/John Knox Press

Book design by
Kristen Dietrich
Appendix developed by Carol Rose Ikler
First United States edition

Published by Westminster/John Knox Press
Louisville, Kentucky

This book is printed on acid-free paper that meets the American National
Standards Institute Z39.48 standard. ∞

PRINTED IN THE UNITED STATES OF AMERICA
2   4   6   8   9   7   5   3

Library of Congress Cataloging-in-Publication Data

Sinclair, Donna, 1943–
    Christian parenting : raising children in the real world / Donna
Sinclair and Yvonne Stewart. — 1st U.S. ed.
        p.   cm.
    ISBN 0-664-25290-7

    1. Parenting—Religious aspects—Christianity.   2. Child rearing—
Religious aspects—Christianity.   3. Children—Religious life.
I. Stewart, Yvonne.   II. Title.
BV4529.S44 1992
649'.7—dc20   91-36612

Dedication

To David, Andy, Tracy, Nancy and Bryan,
and to all the world's children
whose presence fills us with the understanding
that it is God's wish
the world should go on.

CONTENTS

FOREWORD

Through the years, it has been our loss in the United States that a host of significant books have been published in Canada but have never found their way across the border. Thus, with delight and anticipation, I accepted the invitation to read and perhaps write a brief introduction for a U.S. edition of a Canadian book. Moreover, as the author of *Bringing Up Children in the Christian Faith,* I was intrigued by the title *Christian Parenting: Raising Children in the Real World.* I was not disappointed.

Few would question the contention that the raising of children today confronts parents with many serious problems. Raising children as *Christians* confronts parents with many more. Of course, our children have the burden of responsibility to decide for or against the Christian way of life, but they can only do that if we provide them with a faithful witness. Regretfully, there have been far too few good books that help parents do so. Now, thanks to Donna Sinclair and Yvonne Stewart, members of the United Church of Canada, we have one. Both women survived the child-rearing years, one as a mother in a two-career family and the other as a single parent. They courageously chose to reflect on their lives as parents and share their learnings.

Among the many values of their musings are the authors' insights. Far too much of the literature on Christian faith and nurture has been written by men from a masculine perspective. This fact becomes particularly serious when we realize that our perceptions or images of God significantly influence how we behave as parents and relate to our children. Faithful to scripture and the best of Christian tradition, the authors' female perspective is illuminating; their suggestions for child rearing are consistent with their theology.

Through a delightful blend of personal experience and theological reflection the authors engage a variety of complex issues and controversial subjects. While offering no authoritarian pronouncements and having no expectations of agreement, Sinclair and Stewart provide a sensitive, balanced set of insights and implications in terms of concrete, realistic, practical suggestions for being Christian with our children. Their style is easy both to read and to understand. The few "Canadianisms" the reader encounters do not get in the way of the message; indeed, they enhance and enliven it.

Most important, Sinclair and Stewart acknowledge how difficult it is to be Christian in our day, how challenging it is to live in-but-not-of-this-world, and therefore how extremely difficult it is to parent faithfully. They also provide us with content to reflect on, a process for reflection, and the motivation to do so. The fine study guide that accompanies the book turns it into an excellent resource for parent discussion groups. *Christian Parenting* is a book I wish I had written. Even more, I wish I had read and heeded its sage advice as a young parent. (My children might agree!) So read on; I'm convinced you will be grateful that you did.

THE REV. DR. JOHN H. WESTERHOFF
Professor of Theology and Christian Nurture,
The Divinity School, Duke University
Director, Saint Bartholomew's Institute
for Pastoral Studies, Atlanta, Georgia

INTRODUCTION

What parent would ever *dare* write a book about parenting? That thought crossed our minds from time to time as the two of us wrote this book. Any readers who know us could complain that we were entirely out of line. They know our children to be far from perfect.

It's true. Our children—Yvonne has two, Donna has three, and they range in age from ten to twenty-five—are not by any means perfect. But then, no humans at any age are ever perfect. That includes parents; that includes us.

So you should know who we are, and why we risked it.

1. We wrote it out of a belief that God loves all of us in spite of our lack of perfection. That is one of the most remarkable, surprising and endearing of God's qualities; it gave us the courage—some would say *chutzpah*—required.

2. Although our children are not perfect, we do think that somehow—by trial and error, by education, by thought, and sometimes by terrified prayer—we have learned some things that might be of help to other parents raising children.

   Between us, we have a wide range of experience. One of us is a divorced, single mother; one of us is in a busy two-career marriage. Both of us have worked full-time at demanding jobs outside our homes. Both of us took some years off (sort of) to be at home with little kids. Both of us are, at the time of writing, freelancers with flexible hours. Both of us have written widely about children's issues. One of us spent almost eight years as the head of children's work in the national office of a large denomination; one of us writes and edits for children as part of her work.

We have survived our child-rearing, in part, because we are members of a Christian community, and we aren't afraid to draw on that community for support.

Furthermore, it is fair to say that our children have some very useful, even crucial, attributes: they know how to make their own choices and they have a sense of justice.

3. Our most important reason for daring to take this on is our desire to help parents make the connection between the everyday process of parenting and their faith. We believe very strongly that the way parents raise children is inextricably bound up with their theology. If we view God as a stern judge, and base our theology on a punishment model ("If you're not good, you won't get to Heaven") our parenting will reflect that.

But if we view God as a loving co-creator, then our parenting will reflect that attitude, too. We must encourage our children to think for themselves; everyone has responsibility for helping a family function well together.

We think there has been a gap in books about parenting with "Christian" in the title. We have picked up books about Christian parenting and generally put them down again. The ones that have come our way seem heavy with the first view of God: strong on punishment with a great fondness for children who are unquestioningly obedient.

Our book, we hope, reflects the second view of God. The God we write about is not so much the one who flooded the earth, having given up on its inhabitants, but the one who sent a rainbow as recognition that the flood wasn't the only way of doing things. Our God is not a "he," with the sense of patriarchy and hierarchy that resides in that pronoun, but simply God. Our God is not about punishment, but about giving us the freedom of choice which inevitably leads to suffering some consequences for our actions. Our God expects us to share the work of creation—a particularly scary thought when creation is in such trouble.

If our picture of God is a model for our parenting, then that means we are searching out new ways of parenting that are less "being on top," and more cooperative; less "Daddy knows best," and more "solving this problem together"; less about being good and obeying the rules, and more about healing and justice for all.

And that's, finally, why we have written this book—to offer a different but still scriptural view of God. This view calls us to be parents in ways that are in the world but not of it, and to support others who are trying to do the same. Even as we say that, we recognize that we are both irredeemably middle-class, white, university-educated parents; we both have middle-class, white, university-educated aspirations and expectations. We have tried to struggle with the way our milieu affects our values and our beliefs, but we know that that is and always will be a struggle. We simply do our best to remain conscious and questioning.

It's good for parents to know they are not alone. It's hard to help our children live simply, when we live in a society that values people for what they possess, rather than who they are; it's hard to teach them acceptance when our society cherishes winners so highly; and it's hard to teach them tenderness when the idea of sexuality as a God-given gift is so different from what we see in our media. It's not easy to face up to conflict and love our enemies at the same time; and it's not especially "in" to be associated with a church, to be part of the body of Christ.

Don't think we have always—or even most of the time—

succeeded! But as we reflected on how we had tried to raise our children, we realized that that's what we reached for. And sometimes, to our surprise and wonder and delight, we have discovered that our children have learned well, and gone beyond us.

In any case, we aren't presenting you with a strict formula for raising your children. We hope our stories and faith reflections will encourage you to probe your own faith more deeply, and to find the spiritual and practical resources that will help you raise your children in a way congruent with your own vision, and your own faith.

Acknowledgments:

So many people are part of this book for us. It would be impossible to list all the teachers who listened to our children, and heard even the questions that were under the questions, and did their best to answer them. It would be impossible to list all the relatives, the friends, the swim coaches, the church school teachers, the hockey coaches, the directors of plays, and the elders of the community.

But here are a few, a representative sampling, we could call it, of people who have helped us parent, and taught us much. They are not in any sort of order:

David and Sarah Tector; Ian and Janette MacDonald; Stephanie Tekel; Rose Tekel; Wanda and John Wallace; Diane and Paul Lafrance; Patti, Linnie and Judy Elvidge (in their baby-sitting years); Dianne and Paul Morrison; on the Sinclair side of the writing team, grandparents Frank and Margaret Knapp, and Mildred and Clarence Sinclair; on the Stewart side, grandmothers Hazel Fullerton and Mary Stewart.

CHAPTER ONE

Money, designer jeans, and presents

by Donna Sinclair

I remember my daughter's seventh birthday party. Fourteen of her friends made party hats, sang songs, "went on a lion hunt." But the real joy came when the presents were opened: there were boxes of clothes for her Cabbage Patch doll, and stuffed animals with fur as soft as silk. One of them plays "Love Me Tender" if you push its tummy. There were "My Little Ponies" one after another, plastic pink manes and tails curling out of their boxes.

I remember six-year-old Ben, in a paroxysm of excitement, admonishing everyone to "keep calm, keep calm," so often that none of the attendant adults could help laughing. And there were hot dogs and ice cream and a cake with a hundred Smarties on it.

But all the ponies looked at me with the round brown eyes of Ethiopian children, and the Cabbage Patch clothes were

too tenderly made for a doll. They belonged on a baby,
someone living, needing to be warmed.
What, I wondered, have I done to my child?

How do we avoid wounding our children with excess? Will
they ever unlearn the lesson that a large number of pretty
things will make you happy?

It's not just the birthday parties. At Christmas, shelves and
catalogue stores are stocked to the rafters with G.I. Joes and
Mauler Tanks, Rainbow Brite and Care Bear Cousins. Everyone already has a Care Bear, so something new to want has to
be devised. Last year, when everyone already had a Cabbage
Patch doll, their maker packaged them by two and sold them
as Cabbage Patch Twins.

At Easter, the bunny brings new clothes, as well as the
obligatory chocolate eggs and small stuffed rabbits. At
Halloween, people give away candy and chips with cheerful
abandon, while parents make peace with the dentist just in
time for the candy canes of Christmas.

Adolescence creates new problems. Weaned from Cabbage
Patches and Gobots, now tapes of the latest groups, ghetto
blasters on which to play them, and running shoes which
masquerade as art forms become *de rigeur*.

It would be easy to condemn all this outright. But it's much
more complicated than that. Look again at that birthday party.
Mingled with the rank commercialism were real children
taking real pleasure in their friend's good fortune. These
children wish very much to give something that their friend
will love. Hence the fixation on Care Bears. It is a celebration
of the naming day, the day their friend came into the world.

How do we preserve that joy in giving and that profound
sense of ritual without initiating them irrevocably into the
rites of a materialistic society? The distinction is important.
Otherwise those children may never expect to be happy
without similar excess.

We could begin by looking at what gives meaning to our

lives: our theology. Here is the problem as it is stated by
Mark's gospel:

> As Jesus was starting on his way, a man ran up, knelt
> before him, and asked him, "Good Teacher, what must
> I do to receive eternal life?"
>
> "Why do you call me good?" Jesus asked him. "No
> one is good except God alone. You know the com-
> mandments: 'Do not commit murder; do not commit
> adultery; do not steal; do not accuse anyone falsely; do
> not cheat; respect your father and your mother.'"
>
> "Teacher," the man said, "ever since I was young, I
> have obeyed all these commandments."
>
> Jesus looked straight at him with love and said,
> "You need only one thing. Go and sell all you have
> and give the money to the poor, and you will have
> riches in heaven; then come and follow me." When
> the man heard this, gloom spread over his face, and
> he went away sad, because he was very rich.
>
> (Mark 10:17–22, *Good News Bible*)

The story tells us there are other things in life besides a
new VCR. The rich young man made every choice correctly,
except the one about the highest value. He honored his
parents, lived righteously, was true to his family. But when
offered a choice between his money and the chance to live
and work with the greatest teacher and prophet of all time, he
opted for the money. Vision, imagination, the intangible
possibility of a new world—all lost out to the concreteness of
the gold in his pocket.

We don't have to make the same mistake. We can allow
ourselves and our offspring to dream dreams. We can treasure
the ways imaginations flourish, as a way of separating ourselves from a society caught up in its affection for wealth.
This will allow rituals like the flaming birthday cake, the un-
naming and re-naming at Halloween, the promise concealed
in the Easter egg, the growing glow of the Advent wreath,

even grace before meals, to flourish and gain new meaning.

But how? Don't just shrug and give up. There are some helpful principles we can follow.

Young children

Active creation instead of passive consumption

This principle simply means that as often as possible we substitute paint and paper instead of the Masters of the Universe, and glue, scissors, wool, cardboard, empty boxes, clay and playdough instead of Barbie and Ken. We give our children empty packing crates, nails, lumber and mud (space outdoors permitting) instead of fancy little playhouses advertised in the department stores.

Barbie and Ken, in addition to being sexist fluff, are unchangeable. You can dress them up in different outfits but they are immutably tiny, curiously-shaped creatures whose lives are subject to a limited number of plots. Someone sneaked a Barbie and Ken coloring book into our house one day. It was all about how Barbie and Ken go on a series of dates. But you can't imagine them doing anything else. If they went exploring in the jungle, they would get their clothes dirty.

In the same way, the Gobots which change shape to become weapons are simply used to re-enact the wars in which they indulge on television. They can't become anything but their other form. The child's imagination is severely limited. Similarly, toys like Captain Power and Motomonsters, based on television shows, leave little to the child's own mind.

On the other hand, a pile of empty boxes can become anything: a train, maybe, in which the child can actually sit. Add a blanket, and a box becomes a house. Or if the child insists on being aggressive—old habits die hard—it can be a fort; sometimes children do have to fend off the forces of evil. To create something more permanent, the child can use paints, markers or chalk to draw wheels, or an oven door, on a box.

Note that the first thing that has actually *cost* anything in this scenario is the paint. We are used to celebrating our joy in someone's birthday by buying something. So our children will probably scream and say no if we offer to send them to the next birthday party with a pile of empty boxes.

But we can buy a box of paints for a birthday present. Or a pile of wonderful new paper: colored paper, shiny paper, foil paper, tissue paper, carbon paper—the possibilities for entertainment in a sheet of carbon paper, a couple of paper clips, and a hard pencil boggle the mind. (If you aren't getting a birthday present, but just need paper, you can hike down to your local newspaper and get the end of a roll. Costs nothing.) You can encourage your children to make a birthday card for the party. And you can hope that someone in the birthday household appreciates its worth, and says so.

It's also important to model the principle of creativity rather than passivity in our own adult lives. It will be difficult for a child to grasp the notion of active creativity if adult recreation consists of flopping comatose on the couch in front of a TV sitcom. Some of our best memories are of playing charades. Sometimes grown-ups and children played together; sometimes only grown-ups played, while small, astonished children peered from the stairs. A friend remembers the time he made his son a boat from two cardboard boxes; it became the most played with, least expensive toy in that family's history. Cooking, carpentering, going to the theatre together—all those can be activities which nourish the life of the imagination.

Talk with them about the world

To discuss world events with your children, you have to know something yourself about refugees, Central America, South Africa, peace issues. They may hear something about these issues if they attend church school. Let them connect what-went-on-in-Sunday-school-today with your own knowledge, while you sit together around the dinner table or go walking somewhere.

Better not to preach, but just quietly let this happen.

One of our children said once, "You know, it's not that my friends don't care about the Third World. It's that they don't know anything about it." In many churches, you can't help knowing. Share that knowledge—and the hope and vision of inhabitants of the developing world—with your children.

Or go there. One family I know has just returned from a five-month stay in India and Thailand. All of them together. Now they know what many in North America lose sight of— that we are all one family, and we need each other.

Celebrate the products of their imaginations

You can make sure everything your children achieve is valued in *your* home. The fridge, for example, always looks better with a painting stuck to it with tape or magnets. Some of their art could be framed and hung in the living-room, so the children can understand that you value created things above mass-produced things. It will look wonderful—trust me! Children's art is as vital and important as adults', although it may have different qualities.

Give them a chance to be creative with their hands. This is a theological task, after all. We glimpse the mind of God by coming to understand the dilemmas of creation. Our little clay models won't do exactly as we wish. They slip and slide and slump. The playdough we want to preserve cracks in the oven. The paint races over the paper with a life of its own, and the crooked sun with the glasses perched on its nose (all is possible if you are in charge of the universe) looks the way *it* wants, not the way we ordain.

But sometimes, of course, we are well pleased.

Give them books

Just as important is the creation of new universes in children's minds. This feeds the visions they put on paper, lets them escape from the mundane, and introduces them to a thousand new characters who will enrich them.

And—once more—it frees them from the constraints of the yuppie kingdom. If all around them are people who live in neat houses and ride ten-speed bikes, they need to meet the characters of, say, Catfish Bend: Old Doc Raccoon, telling stories and collecting dimes, and Judge Black, the old snake who has become wise and vegetarian.

Give the child a library card. Fill the house with borrowed picture books. For yourself, read Michelle Landsberg's wonderful, passionate _Guide to Children's Books_ (Penguin) and her remarks on how to allow children to love reading, even with parents who aren't book-lovers themselves. "Children's literature," says Landsberg, "offers an almost magical opportunity to non-reading adults to begin again, and to discover the pleasures of reading along with their children."

You don't accomplish this miracle by using flashcards at the age of three. You do it by reading aloud, and hugging your children as you read, and enjoying the book as much as they do. And by mentioning, when Auntie Joan wants to buy the child something special, the name of that new book by Robert Munsch or Monica Hughes or John Bianchi.

Vision of _Shalom_

With all these suggestions—literary, visual, musical, tactile—you open up for the child the vision of an alternate universe, one that is different and more hopeful than the one we inhabit. It's one of the tasks of art.

It can also free us from the dependence on things which afflicts our generation. Art allows us to envision a world where a person's worth is not measured by possessions. Our children have no need for battery-powered airplanes and cars when their toys are propelled by their imaginations. It is imagination, you see, that Mark's rich man missed out on. And he lost more than he knew. He lost the sense that things could be more just than they are. He never caught the vision of a peaceable Kingdom where we are at one with our surroundings and no one is hungry.

Finally, we can talk with our children about their visions and dreams for the world. What do they think the world should be like? How do they hope it will be when they grow up? How would they fix things? American theologian Walter Brueggemann points out how the Old Testament prophets continually forced their hearers first to look at reality, and then to dream of possibility. Our children, in their innocence, often do the same thing. By their questions, they force us to see things the way they really are—and find ways to imagine something different.

Northrop Frye explains in his classic, *The Educated Imagination* (CBC), that something is crucial to our humanity: "If we shut the vision of it completely out of our minds, or insist on its being limited in various ways, something goes dead inside us, perhaps the one thing that's really important to keep alive."

What goes dead is the *Shalom*, God's world of peace and justice. And it is an elusive and marvellous concept. Children need it, even though it is hard for them to understand. It is what Jesus came to bring us. It is here, sometimes, in glimpses, when people are kind to one another; and not-yet-here, when we are cruel.

We can't let Gobots and television, batteries and store-bought dreams, shut that vision of *Shalom* out of our children's minds.

Teenagers

The day comes when your children no longer create art to put on the fridge. The question of whether to watch television or make monsters out of playdough no longer arises. Your children have become adolescents.

They may, at this time, seem faintly scandalized with you and your values. They may question the choices you have made in life, especially if you don't have an income sufficient to their wants. And they will want things in a way you hadn't dreamed possible. Names like Ralph Lauren and Polo (you always thought that was a game played on horseback by the idle rich, didn't you?) take on new significance. This can be painful, especially if "all the other kids" have a lot of clothes or easy access to one of the family cars, when your family may be driving only one car, and it's rusting.

Until then, you may have gotten away with a casual approach to money, or with paying a small monthly allowance. Not any more.

Peer pressure

Part of the problem is that the time has arrived when the children must begin in earnest to form their own identity, separate from the family in which they grew up. This is a necessary and extremely important step. They must now question every single value of their parents, everything they have accepted more or less comfortably until now. But, since this is a dangerous task, they need support. Nobody can stand alone. So their friends and classmates become more crucial to them than ever before.

There is nothing wrong with this. Their friends' affirmation is necessary and healthy. But it can be scary for you, especially if you're not sure you like all of your children's friends.

In addition, teenage subculture is permeated by a strong sense that we are what we wear. (So are a lot of adult subcultures. Look thoughtfully at your own.) So if a certain (expensive) kind of jeans is in, not to wear them is to be excluded from the culture. Invisible.

The task then becomes one of negotiating between the values of the teen subculture and your own values as a family within the church. Your values say, I hope, that there are other things in life than appearances—things like compassion, and hope, and everybody in the world having a fair share.

This is not easy to negotiate.

Now is the time to build on the trust you have developed

with your kids during the first 12 years of their life. Even if you're not sure you've developed that trust, and your children are now 13, 14 or 15, it's not too late to start.

One important component is discussion time. You can't find your values in the midst of the surrounding culture if you never talk with the kids to explain why you do things the way you do, and what it means to be Christian and "*in* but not *of* the world."

This may require you to do some thinking of your own. Maybe you *do* completely subscribe to the values of the culture around you. If so, why are you reading this book? It assumes that to be Christian is to be different in some ways. This doesn't mean that everything society values is bad, nor that we are unthinkingly trapped in society's values. We can choose. Even the act of going to church is increasingly countercultural, more and more an act of conscious choice.

Nor does it mean you have to wear a hair shirt. In an old family diary I found the minutes of a family council meeting from September 17, 1979. The minutes are brief and to the point:

> New Business: Andy wants color TV and cable.
> Cost: $25 cable installation. $9.50 x 12 (monthly
> cost) = $102. Color TV itself = $350 or more.
> David says we need good clear reception. Mom says
> TV OK but wants us outside in nice weather. Decided
> Andy will study prices this week.
> Adjourned.

It's a pretty short notation. We were never very good at formal family councils, although we do discuss things. But you can see the negotiating of values going on. Mom values being outside and getting exercise (something she doesn't do well herself, actually, but no one really challenged her on that point.) The children would like to see Mr. Dress-up clearly, not in a black and white snowstorm.

We ended up with a new TV (actually, Nannie gave it to

the family for Christmas). *And* cable hookup (from us). Nobody turned into a couch potato. And as far as I know, we haven't slid irrevocably into materialism.

But, in the process, the children learned that it's important to figure out *why* you are doing something. They learned that you don't *have* to follow society's rule in everything without discussion ("but everyone has a color TV!"). They were also reminded that their wishes had some weight in family discussions.

So cling to your values and your sanity, and do your best to let your children have theirs.

In addition to talking things over with them, these few catch phrases may continue to be useful, even if you only whisper them, late at night, to your partner or to the wall:

It's all right to want things; everybody wants things sometimes. Confess, you want things too. Wouldn't all your music sound better on a compact disc player? Wouldn't a microwave oven be a great convenience? We won't necessarily get all those things we want. Better, if your child moans about how everyone else is wearing designer jeans, to be sympathetic and acknowledge their feelings. ("You'd really like those jeans, wouldn't you?") At the same time, you hold up reality for them. ("But we can't afford them this pay cheque," or, "Maybe you could do some babysitting.")

We are all responsible for our own actions. Sometimes the desire for the jeans or the new Walkman or the latest record is so strong that all of Grandma's birthday money, or the babysitting money, or their whole allowance, goes into buying that item—to your chagrin, since you think it could have been more responsibly spent in other ways. Grit your teeth and say nothing. The only way they'll learn to suffer the consequences of their actions is to suffer them. Freezing in December because they didn't save enough of their clothing allowance for a new ski jacket teaches a lot about cause and effect.

It may lead them to discover second-hand clothing stores—an enormously freeing experience.

They may see an after-school job as a solution. Having a job can solve a lot of problems. They can then make their own decisions about the designer jeans. But again, discuss this decision carefully *with* them, without making the decision *for* them. Will the time needed for the job hurt their marks? Are they willing to give up a part in the school play in order to make enough money to buy the latest albums?

You can voice other criteria than simply making money. This may be when you explain why you chose the job you did, what factors led you to spend your life doing one thing instead of another. Money? Job satisfaction? If you gave up your dream of a new Audi every three years in order to do something you loved, this may be something they need to hear.

The point is simple: they should feel free enough, on one hand, not to be *owned* by money, and on the other, to earn enough to be in charge of some things that matter to them. Independence, separation, and identity are all wrapped up in this. It's tricky.

We all have a right, as much as possible, to make our own choices, even if later they turn out to be wrong. Like one child who—growing up—determined to put away childish things and put his beloved collection of stuffed animals in the Salvation Army bin. His mother, suffering over this same loss of childhood, allowed this act of generosity, and sympathized when he later regretted it. It hurt. But there will be other choices in life, also painful; other times that they will regret what they have done. It's good to practice when they are young; it makes it easier to live with those decisions later on.

Good models continue to be important. Children—of whatever age—do notice how we spend our money, what we value. Witness the following exchange, which took place in our household, the year we went into feeding the birds in a big way.

Visitor: (eyeing several hundred grosbeaks, devouring an enormous pile of seeds from the feeders on the front lawn). What *is* your father feeding all those birds?

Andy: (at age thirteen, not a bird-lover) My college education.

Despite Andy's rueful reply, he recognizes he is a member of a family in which money sometimes goes for things that offer no tangible return. That same son, startled one day to observe what we gave to the church, and mentally computing the number of ten-speed bikes and stereos that money might have bought, made no complaint. The idea of struggling to be a reasonably good steward is part of the atmosphere of our house, and one which he accepts.

That's because of considerable grace which exists in our house around the issue of money as well. It's not one we have licked, this question. But we do tend to share with one another. Along with suffering the consequences of not saving enough for the winter jacket may come the unexpected gift of one during the January sales. And there is a sure sense that— despite feeding the birds—everyone's college education, if that's what they want, is important enough for the parents to make sacrifices.

We're trying to say, by these examples, that it is possible to be in the world and not of it, as long as you don't get your whole identity from material things. One isn't doomed for wearing a Polo T-shirt. But it is important for children to know why they feel that particular shirt is necessary—and to know that they are worthy of esteem even without these accoutrements.

Take heart. There will come a surprising day when your children emerge from adolescence. It occurs just before they leave home. Ironically, now that you have managed to raise reasonably pleasant adults, you are deprived of them.

However, you may also find that you have raised children who base their lives on something other than how rich they can become, who prize imagination over acquisition, and who can envision and work for a better world.

You may have children who take delight in sharing what they have with others. That characteristic offers great potential for happiness. Most of all, you may have children who won't make the same mistake as the rich man described in Mark's gospel, who let his riches come between him and full life, who "went away very sad, because he was very rich."

CHAPTER TWO

Competition, getting ahead, or going together

by Yvonne Stewart

Almost as soon as my first child, Nancy, was born, the competition was on. I was forever being asked "How much did she weigh?" or "How long was she?" Then I had to listen to a comparison of her statistics to cousin Jane's baby or friend Anne's.

Later came other questions. "Is she eating solids yet? Has she got her first tooth? Is she walking yet? Has she said her first word?" And again the inevitable comparisons to note whether she was ahead of or behind other babies her age.

My stomach still knots up when I think of those conversations. I never liked that game, and avoided it at all costs. In fact (to my regret, now) I refused even to keep records of those milestones in my children's lives, because of the prevalent sense of competition. Of course, I wanted my children to thrive and do well. That's part of being a parent. But I didn't want their growth and development to be constantly assessed as "better than" or "worse than" the neighbor's child.

When my son Bryan grew older, I also avoided attending his minor league hockey games as much as possible. On those occasions when I did go, I saw and heard parents screaming insults at their children for making mistakes, and shouting at them to "kill" their opponents (or at least maim them). And I saw children in tears at the end of a game, not only because they lost but because they knew they faced further abuse from the coach and their parents in the dressing room. I stayed away because I felt powerless to do anything about this fierce competitiveness. Now, in retrospect, I think maybe I could have done something, but then I chose to stay away.

The pros and cons of competition

I struggled with the pros and cons of competition long before I became a parent, but parenthood pushed me into the middle of this tension.

On the one hand, I felt instinctively that this kind of competition did not fit with my Christian understanding of how community was supposed to function.

On the other hand, I was taught at church that I was supposed to make the best use of my talents. That meant doing well. Which in turn meant getting good marks and prizes in competition against others—for academic, athletic or artistic ability. Competing for and winning a scholarship to university for high marks, or winning an event in the Olympics, was a "good" thing to do.

When I became a parent, I worried about how to help my children develop their abilities to their fullest, as I had been taught, without making them feel like failures if they didn't win prizes or come first in competition with others.

Parent-teacher meetings at my children's two different high schools gave me some insights into competition and the motivation behind it. Bryan started out in the high school in our neighborhood—an apartment community made up of sub-sidized·and middle-class housing, populated by people from 57 nations. Bryan's school usually had a good, but not over-whelming, turnout for parent-teacher meetings. The parents were often well-educated, but some, because of their immi-grant or refugee status, had menial jobs. They were coopera-tive, even subservient to the teachers. Their chief concern was whether their children were learning enough and working hard enough.

Nancy wanted to study Russian. So she went to the nearest school that offered the subject. It was in a largely white, middle-class neighborhood. Nancy's school had such a crush of parents I had to arrive two hours before interviews began to get appointments with the teachers my daughter wanted me to see. Here, many parents acted as if the teachers were their servants. The parents' main concern was whether their child-ren were getting top marks; they often implied that teachers needed to shape up to make sure this happened.

The young people at both schools were under pressure to compete. Those from the immigrant or lower middle-class families were expected to excel because, as part of a minority group, they had to get "good" jobs. Parents wanted their children to earn a decent living, to have self-respect, and, if possible, to avoid being treated as second rate.

The youth at Nancy's school were under pressure to maintain the social status quo. They had to do well to get into the "right" universities, to succeed in the professions that would maintain their family's status in their social class.When Bryan's friend, Paul, failed his last year of high school, his well-to-do parents told him how ashamed they were. They had to admit to their friends at the club that he wasn't going to the chosen university after all.

Competition as a power issue

The competition within both these groups of students was for _power_. The students at Bryan's school had to do well to *acquire* power—earning power—to survive. The other students had to be on top to *keep* power.

Competition seems to operate on the assumption that power is finite. If people believe there is only so much power to go around, then those who have it, whether in sports or academics or politics, have to hold on to it for all they're worth. And those who don't have enough power fight to take some away from someone else. And those who don't have any power at all are held down, discriminated against, oppressed so they cannot use or get power.

Are winners "good," and losers "bad"?

There seems to be an implicit understanding: those who win must be "good" and those who lose are "bad." In team sports, for example, the struggle to win is often portrayed as a metaphor for the struggle of good over evil. On television, born-again athletes declare, "God answered our prayers and gave us victory," as if God were on their side and not on the side of the losing team. Home town enthusiasm cheers the local team as "the good guys," the visitors as an enemy.

But the syndrome isn't limited to sports. We see television preachers implying that God gives material wealth and prosperity (which gives people status in our competitive society) to those who follow them. Therefore, those who don't have wealth aren't right with God.

Our society pursues a similar pattern of thinking, when it blames the poor for being poor—implying that they made a bad choice. By being lazy instead of hard-working in the competitive business world, they chose to be poor.

What does our faith say?

I didn't want my children to have this view of "losers." Nor did I want them to live their lives competing for power and status.

Where do our Judeo-Christian teachings fit into all of this? Well, first of all, those teachings don't agree with the underlying assumption of competition—that power is finite and has to be hoarded. The biblical story teaches us that God graciously shares power. Firstly with God's people, but _all_ people have equal access to God's power. (Note that I say _access_ not _quantity_.) When the Hebrew slaves cried out in their pain of Egyptian oppression, God led them to a land of their own and granted them power in their own lives. God gave this power to the Hebrews because they agreed to be God's covenant people. Being God's covenant people meant following God's rules—such as not coveting or competing for each other's goods, returning land and possessions to debtors in due time, giving one tenth of one's goods for the benefit of others. The emphasis was on ensuring the well-being of _every_ member of the community, rather than on competing for first place in terms of power, status and material goods.

There are some threads through the Old Testament which imply that God _blesses_ the chosen people with physical and material well-being, and punishes by withholding prosperity. But the focus is really on _blessings_, on gifts from God, that were not originally deserved or earned. The focus is also on the necessity of sharing with others not so blessed, because God also cares about them.

When the Hebrew people did not follow these rules of God, they understood that God was furious. Before the Hebrew people were sent into exile, their prophets called upon them to save themselves from God's anger, to care for widows and orphans and strangers, to share economic resources, to ensure that justice was done. Jesus similarly called people to repent, to change, to live as if God's rules were obeyed throughout the world—to live as if God's kingdom or community were right here, right now.

Jesus was aware of the competitive grabbing for power in his times. When his disciples were jostling for a place of honor, he told them that in order to be the greatest in God's eyes, they must be last in society's. They must be like children or servants who have no power. His stories of God's kingdom often pointed out that those who appeared to be the least deserving in their competitive society—such as the prodigal son and the late-arriving workers in the vineyard—were just as deserving in God's eyes as everyone else. These "least" were certainly no more good or evil than anyone else.

Jesus shocked those with power and status in his community by associating with outcasts—lepers, prostitutes, Samaritan women, tax collectors, adulterers—and by selecting as his disciples fishermen rather than learned rabbis. He acted out his conviction that God was with these people as much as anyone else.

In other words, people didn't have to compete to be close to God. Paul emphasized this too, in his letter to the Romans (11:6); he affirmed that God loves everyone without anyone having to earn that love.

Jesus also taught about using our abilities. The money in the parable of the talents is often taken to represent the gifts God has given us (Matthew 25:14–30). If we put this story in the context of the rest of Jesus' teaching, clearly those who follow Jesus are to use both their God-given talents and their money for the sake of others as well as themselves.

So what do we do?

These biblical reflections led me to feel that I had to try to live my vision of what God's world could be like. Then I could invite my children to join me. Instead of fostering an individualistic get-ahead-of-the-others atmosphere, we should live in community, as part of God's people, valuing all people and giving them the opportunity to develop their talents and well-being as best they can.

But how? How do we live as if the community of God were here now, even though we know it isn't? Even when we are surrounded by a competitive hierarchical society that keeps children, women, natives, the disabled and minority groups as low on the ladder as possible?

As Christians, God expects us to develop our gifts so that

we can act _with_ God, as Jesus did, to help the oppressed in
our society get enough power to take responsibility for their
own lives. If we are members of oppressed groups, then, we
have to claim our share of power. If we're a privileged group,
we don't compete to get more power, or to hold on to more
than our share.

We are also required to live in this world but not of it. We
and our children can't avoid participating in a competitive
society. But we can do so with a different motivation. We
don't do it to beat others. We compete, not to be better than
others, or to gain power over others, but to acquire our share
of power or to help others get theirs. Daughters still may have
to compete to become engineers or business managers.
Parents can support them, not to "get ahead" but to make the
way easier for other women to follow, and so that these
daughters can use their talents to contribute new dimensions
to engineering or business.

About competitive sports

What if your child has the talent to participate in competitive team or individual sports such as hockey or gymnastics,
and is really keen to do so? You know that these are intensely
competitive fields. You worry that your child might be hurt
by not doing well, or may be coached according to cut-throat
values that you disagree with. What do you do?

I would let my child participate. But I would also make
sure I discussed my perspective with the child and the coach
so that they both know there are different points of view
about athletic competition. Competition with good players
can help children learn new skills or refine old ones. And that
can be _fun_.

In my son's hockey playing days, I know I didn't convey
to him that watching a game was fun. I'm sure I looked
miserable those few times I attended, sitting in the stands
surrounded by the noise and trappings of a battleground. But I
could relax about the results of the game. My son knew he

would rate just as highly in my eyes whether the team won or lost. And he knew I would never hang over the boards berating him for his mistakes.

If your child gets involved in a sport where you find the coaching methods and intense emphasis on competition destructive, perhaps you could try to change things. Once, at a hockey camp Bryan was attending, I observed a coach. During the demonstration game for parents, he stood beside the goalie, berating him with comments supposed to incite the boy to play better. "You're the stupidest kid I've ever coached," he yelled. "You haven't learned a thing here, have you? I can't believe you just did that! That was terrible."

When I expressed my concern to the coach, he didn't have the slightest idea of what I was talking about. I failed to make my point. But *you* may have the interest or ability to help coach the team, to put your principles into practice. Then you can ensure all children get coached well and have a chance to play.

Sometimes one parent's voice isn't enough. Perhaps you can find others who will form a group, and ask the officials of the organization to change its emphasis from combative competition to team work and skill development for the enjoyment of all.

If this doesn't work—and if your child is enjoying playing—don't give up or withdraw; explore alternatives. For example, there are semi-organized pick-up shinny games in public rinks, where everyone gets a turn and the purpose is to *play*. There are athletic clubs where young people get together to have fun at their favorite sports. If such organizations don't exist in your area, perhaps you could get help to set something up.

We parents need to counter the atmosphere of high pressure competitiveness in our children's sports activities. Our bodies, minds and spirits are gifts from God which we are to cherish and enjoy, not damage and punish in order to be better than someone else or to be a "winner."

God loves us, with all our shortcomings. Children should receive that message in all aspects of life, and especially in athletic activities, which are meant to be recreative and refreshing.

As Christians, we are part of God's people, not just separate individuals. Therefore we are required to work for the well-being of all. Children should be able to play sports in a manner that allows them to consider their teammates, enabling all to enjoy the pleasure of the game and of doing well. Being encouraged to cheat, or to hurt players on the other team in order to win, does not help our children share power. Nor does it contribute to the quality of community life.

Discerning and developing children's talents

Sometimes competition helps children learn what their talents and gifts are, and how to use them well.

I remember a calf-judging at the Royal Winter Fair. The calf owners were boys and girls about 12–14 years old. They had carefully raised their animals and brought them to the fair, hoping to win a prize. The judge handled the competition with the attitude that all these young people were trying to learn how to raise the best cattle possible, to feed the most people well. He explained why each calf had won in a way that helped all the participants learn from each other's experience. They felt that they were in the people-feeding business together. I'm sure the children who didn't get a prize were disappointed. But they weren't humiliated. And they learned how to do a better job of raising cattle. Or, perhaps, they learned that they weren't cut out for cattle raising.

As a young teen, I dreamed of being a gymnast. But once I joined the high school gym club and practiced with others, I quickly realized I did not have a gift for the sport. It was a painful but necessary discovery. Children need to learn what their God-given gifts are and to develop them. They will only frustrate themselves and others by trying to nurture talents that aren't there.

As your children cast about to see what their talents and interests are—taking piano, dancing, or painting lessons, joining groups for stamp collecting, Scouts, Brownies—look for a teacher or leader with an attitude like the calf judge. The leader's attitude should focus on helping children find and develop their real talents.

This is important. Since our gifts are God-given, we are to use them for God's purposes—not for ours alone. They were not given to us to make ourselves more powerful or more wealthy than others.

And of course, gifts are given to be enjoyed. If you put your children in competitive situations where they can't enjoy their gifts, you put that gift in jeopardy. He or she may choose not to nurture it because it gives no pleasure. That would be a loss to your child and to the others who may have received pleasure from it. I heard of one talented boy who loved hockey, but not high pressure. His father kept shouting at him to "Get in there, son, go get 'em!" One day, in the middle of a power play, the boy skated casually off the rink and refused to play again. He couldn't take it any more.

On the other hand, your child might enjoy expressing his or her gifts in recitals and competitions.

One Christmas, I saw a superb production of "The Nutcracker Suite." I especially enjoyed watching the girl who danced the role of Clara. This young woman was a "winner" in the competitive world of dance. The audience could not know what motivated her. Was it to be better than others? Or to make the best use of her talent so that she and others could enjoy the beauty of her gift? But though the audience might not know, *she* would know. And she would live accordingly—either striving always to be ahead or enjoying and disciplining her gift to serve her art (*service*, the opposite of competition).

I hope her parents were able to help her develop the latter attitude.

Achievement at school

Some people say that competition at school, and in other areas of life, prepares children for the competitiveness of the real world. This may be.

But Christian parents can't let this experience stand alone. Our children have to learn to live in this world; they also need a vision of what it *could* be like. In God's kingdom, people don't need to compete for love, attention, forgiveness, justice, material goods. These are given and shared generously among God's faithful people.

Our children need to know that education contributes to the well-being of individuals and society for its own sake—not just to careers and getting ahead. I didn't win any scholarships. I never stood at the top of my class. I never had a high-powered and high-paying job. Yet my life has been greatly enriched by my education—and I hope my family and community has been too! Our children would function with less tension and more joy if they understood—from us—what a privilege it is to learn, what a pleasure education can bring to life. Then it wouldn't matter if they were at the bottom of the academic competition—as long as they were learning, as long as they were doing their best, without coming under pressure to excel in the race for power.

We need to help our children develop their academic abilities. But we also need to let them know that love doesn't have to be earned. It doesn't depend on doing well. Even if they're brilliant, they are no better and no more valued than brothers and sisters and friends who don't have the same ability.

Children will not get this message if parents wait breathlessly for their report cards, or make a big fuss over the child who stands first in the class while criticizing the one who got average marks. Children may feel that they have to do well academically in order to rate in the family.

Better that each child receive positive feedback for hard work, for teachers' comments, for marks where possible. Our

children need to know that we love them as God does no
matter what their marks. A conversation might go like this:

> **Joyce:** Here's my report card, Mom and Dad.
> **Dad:** (reading it carefully) Joyce, I'm really glad to
> see how hard you worked in math.
> **Joyce:** (pouting) Yeah, but I still got a C.
> **Dad:** Sounds as if you don't feel too happy about it.
> **Joyce:** Well, Tanya got an A.
> **Dad:** It would be nice to get an A, I agree. But the
> teacher said you worked hard and really improved,
> and that's great! Is there something your mom and I
> could do to help you if you really want to do better in
> math?

Choosing the "right" school

Parents often put a lot of thought into where they should
send their children to school. As Christian parents, we need to
examine our motives when we consider this subject. Why
would you want to send your children to a certain private
school or a public school in a different area?

- to give them status and help them make the right
  connections?
- to keep them away from "negative" influences of
  other children—their class, ethnic and racial background, or from drug and alcohol abuse?
- so you won't have to get involved with problems in
  certain schools that might prevent all children from
  getting a good education?

If these are your reasons, they are competitive ones. You
are choosing a school because it makes or keeps your children
better than others.

You might, however, want to send your children to an
alternative school which uses a more just and challenging
style of education in order to show a slow-to-change school
system how it can be done. Your motivation expresses your
values. Christians cannot cop out on the public domain for the

sake of getting our children ahead of others. We are called to work for good education for all children.

I struggled with these issues twice. First my daughter, and then my son, wanted to take subjects not offered locally. Nancy wanted to take Russian and vocal music. Bryan wanted to take art. The only way they could take these subjects was to change to high schools out of our area.

Some middle-class people in our community had chosen not to send their children to the neighborhood high school—even though it had high academic standards—because they did not want their children to be "dragged down" by associating with young people from subsidized housing and from a mix of racial, ethnic and language backgrounds. I felt it was a privilege for my children to be part of such a rich ethnic and class mix. I thought that their attendance at this school was part of our Christian witness. And so I was sorry they had to move to largely white, middle-class schools to take the subjects they wanted.

Career choices: for fulfillment or status?

Almost from the time they can talk, adults ask children what they want to be when they grow up—meaning what job do they want. Often parents influence their children's career choices, consciously or unconsciously, by enrolling them in certain schools and particular extra-curricular activities, or by setting up a savings fund for university.

Parents may find it acceptable for their child at age three or four to want to be a firefighter or a carpenter, but not at 17 or 18. Why? Because parents want their children to do well. Doing well, in our society, means moving up the ladder. A ladder of any kind implies that some jobs rank higher or better than others. Usually white-collar and professional jobs are considered further up the ladder than blue-collar. So the parents—in this case, they could be blue-collar workers themselves—want their child to climb higher on the ladder than a firefighter in order to do well in their eyes. For other parents, becoming a firefighter might represent a step up. And we all know about the proverbial parents who want their children to be doctors—not for any altruistic reasons!

Some parents want their children to follow in their footsteps, carrying on their business or profession. They seek immortality for themselves and their work, not job satisfaction for their children. Others may want their offspring to accomplish what they couldn't. My school friend's brother was zealously pushed by his father to be the professional hockey player his dad couldn't be. Or parents may want their children to get jobs that are sex-role stereotypes. One young man I know is gifted and interested in a career in nursing or geriatrics or early childhood education. But his family and friends feel he must do something more masculine, and more lucrative. He feels paralyzed, caught between the impulses of his God-given gifts and his desire to please. Young women still meet resistance when they attempt to develop their abilities as business executives.

As Christian parents, we need to help our children discover what gifts they have and what careers they suit—whether they are blue-collar or white, high status or low, "feminine" or "masculine," well paid or not. We violate our children when we push them to enter status professions for which they are not suited. If you question that, turn the matter around. Do you want your family treated by a doctor who practices medicine simply because the profession provides status and money? Or would you rather have a doctor who cares about the health and well-being of individuals and communities and has the ability to foster such health? To push our children to compete for careers they aren't suited for damages not only their lives, but the lives of the people they work with and for, and ultimately denies God and God's gifts.

Sharing power at home

But it's not just the world out there that we need to be paying attention to. Christian parents need to demonstrate in

the family, too, that power can be shared without any being
lost. Children need to feel that they have some power over
their own lives and can contribute to family life. They do not
need to have power over others—be they brothers and sisters
or parents!

From the time they are very young, children can participate
in decisions that affect them. For example, instead of deciding
exactly what dress or pants you will buy for your children,
you can let them choose a color or style within a price range
you can afford. If they feel they have some power, they won't
need to compete with you for it—like refusing to wear what
you chose for them. This worked in our family.

Children derive a positive sense of shared power by taking
on responsibilities. They feel needed; they know they have
something to offer others. They may even feel less competitive with brothers and sisters if their gifts are appreciated and
used for the sake of the family.

My son used to love to cook for us (he still does, though it
was more of a thrill for him at age seven or eight) but he
wasn't great at organizing meals. Everything wasn't always
ready at the right time, in the proper dishes, and so on. I could
have put him down for his lack of organization; I could have
belittled his sister for her lack of interest in cooking. Both of
these criticisms would have led to fierce rivalry. Instead, I
asked her to use her gifts of organizing to help her brother
cook. He, in turn, helped feed us. Neither had to prove superi-
ority over the other. They both knew they had strengths and
weaknesses, yet they could work together to accomplish
something.

Sibling rivalry

A friend has two rivalrous daughters. She gets worn down
by the constant refrain she hears: "That's not fair! She got
more than I did!" Many parents with more than one child
know this refrain all too well.

But do you really create equality by giving equal amounts?

Sometimes we parents try to treat children equally to reduce the competition among them. Usually this increases the tension instead. You end up with siblings counting every penny, every item, every minute given by parents to make sure everything is fair.

Our children need to know what we know about God—that they have equal *access* to their parents as we do to God, but the *amount given* in response may vary according to need. (That's why I referred earlier to *access*, not *quantity*.) The elder brother of the prodigal, the workers in the vineyard, the self-righteous Pharisees—all found this a hard lesson in Jesus' time. It's still a difficult one today, but if well learned by our children, it will help them avoid destructive aspects of competition.

Another friend often responds to her son's complaint by saying,

> "You're right, Derek, it isn't fair. But that's the way life is. Natalie is getting a new snowsuit and you're going to have to wear your hand-me-down one for another year. But Natalie has outgrown hers and has no cousin to give her one. So we have to buy her a new one. Someday you'll need something, and we'll have to spend more money for you than for Natalie. The amount we spend doesn't have anything to do with how much we love you."

Our children must know we love them even if a sister gets a great deal more money spent on her braces, or a brother gets a lot more parental help with his homework because he needs it. Then they will be able to accept the seeming inequities without demanding a fair share or putting down siblings. They will know *their* needs will be met when these needs arise.

In some homes, children compete to be the good ones, telling tales about each other to their parents. You can reduce this kind of competition if you refrain from blaming children for their actions. Instead, help them deal with the consequences of their behavior.

My three-year-old neighbor came to visit me recently. She insisted on carrying her glass of juice out to our porch. On the way, she spilled it. She seemed worried about what I would do. I gave her a cloth and suggested she wipe it up. As she wiped, she kept asking, "Are you still my friend, Yvonne?"

"Yes, I am," I replied. She was amazed that I wasn't even mad at her. In her home, she would have been yelled at and sent away while her mother cleaned up. At the same time, her brother would have teased her because he was in his mother's good books and she wasn't. Later, she would get even, when he got into trouble.

If children learn that it's not so terrible to make mistakes, and if they learn to repair the consequences, they won't have the same need to compete with each other. They'll also know something about God's forgiveness. They won't need to project wrongdoing and blame on others because they know they are loved even if they aren't always "good."

Some families handle the problems that arise from competition in the home by having formal family gatherings to work things out. Others deal with things on the fly as they go about their daily routines. Whatever the method, the message needs to be clear: in families, children don't need to compete for power. At the same time, they may need to remind other members of their right to some power from time to time.

This experience will give children an alternate vision of the use of power that works. When children go out into the competitive world of sports, school and work, they will be able to act in less competitive power-sharing ways if they so choose.

Many parenting books explain the complexities of sibling rivalry in light of each child's position in the family—older, middle, younger—and offer practical ways to alleviate friction. These are well worth reading and applying in the light of our Christian values of sharing power, accepting and forgiving as God does.

What if children don't want to compete?

A concerned father once asked me, "How can I get my daughter to pursue her outstanding talent for Scottish country dancing? I've tried everything I can think of to get her to continue her lessons and to participate in competitions. But she still says 'no'. What should I do?"

I suspect this girl may have been turned off by too much pressure. Even if parents back off, or find non-competitive ways for the child to develop, the child may still not budge. Time sometimes helps, though. My daughter has considerable musical talent, but was turned off at age eight after taking piano lessons from a good but competitive, pressuring teacher. She didn't return to piano until she was 17.

Parents can help identify gifts, offer lessons, and give support in competitive situations or alternative non-competitive experience, but parents cannot make their children use their talents, in competition or otherwise. God gives us gifts and the freedom to use them or not. Parents must grant their children the same freedom.

What if children aren't allowed to compete?

Children want to enter some of life's competitions but often aren't considered eligible to do so—not because they lack the gifts but because of who they are.

I remember the anger I felt, reading a newspaper article about a woman's struggle to become and remain a plastic surgeon. She said,

"Because I am a woman, I had a hard time competing to get into this specialty. And when I did get in, I felt I had to prove that I could be as good as, if not better than, men, in my studies and medical practice, and I had to do it their way rather than mine. Even after I proved to be an excellent plastic surgeon, I was still under pressure from my family and friends to give up my work when I had children."

Would this doctor have been made to feel guilty if she were male? No. Being female was what was supposed to determine what she did, not her talents to repair shattered and deformed bodies. Why didn't people suggest her *husband* stay home? Why couldn't they *both* work part-time?

Disabled people, or those of different races or ethnic groups, are often denied entrance to training programs and employment. Their gifts don't matter—their appearance and background does. The loss is society's as well as theirs. That's a sure clue to *harmful* competitiveness—when everyone loses.

Although Jesus is quoted as saying that those who follow him must be servants, he also implied in the story of Lazarus and the rich man (Luke 16:19-31) that those who have been servants in this world will *not* be servants in God's kingdom. Jesus was talking to the people who really were servants—who carried water to the rich. They were servants because of who they were, not because of any lack of gifts. They were foreigners, blacks, poor, disabled, captives, women, children. Think about the people who play the servant roles in our society today. This list hasn't changed much.

Jesus was *not* implying that these servants must endure their position until the afterlife. We are called to live as if God's kingdom or community is here on earth now. In that community, all people can use their God-given gifts appropriately. White, Anglo-Saxon, middle-class people can become house cleaners if that is their talent; poor immigrants can become nuclear scientists. They do what they are gifted for, not what society says they should do because of their class, gender, color or disability.

Some groups have worked together to prove the value of their gifts, rather than competing their way into the existing system. Women who wanted to be doctors formed their own medical schools and hospitals. Blacks and natives also set up separate school systems, or after-school programs where young people could learn about their own history and tradition and develop a sense of self-worth and competence. Ultimately, I think these parents need to help at least some of their children—girls, native, black, disabled—use their talents in mainstream society—for society's sake. Society needs to learn, for example, that someone seriously disabled with cerebral palsy has the ability to counsel *all* people—not just other *similarly disabled* people.

I have two acquaintances—one black and one Hispanic—who managed to get excellent educational training and then teach at the post-graduate level. Both credit their mothers. Under the cloud of constant discrimination, their mothers constantly told them, "You are a child of God. God loves you as much as everyone else and wants blessings in life for you too." With this firm belief in themselves, they never allowed put-downs to discourage them. And, against difficult odds, they developed their talents and used them for the benefit of black and white, Anglo and Hispanic.

These women did compete. But their motivation was to have a fair share of power and to have an opportunity to share their gifts. They didn't compete to be ahead of others or to have more than others.

What if children can't compete?

It's painful as a parent to see your children neglected in games or picked last because they aren't "good enough" to help a team win. You could encourage cooperative games where participants work together to accomplish the goals of the game. But, nevertheless, you, your child and your child's playmates, know that your child is not well coordinated physically.

Or it's heartbreaking to have people stare at your Down's syndrome child, and to have regular school systems reject him or her as a student. Family and friends can enjoy the gifts of love and affection from such a child, but you know that he or she is considered mentally disabled.

I worked on a project with a young man who had cerebral

palsy. He walked with a stagger, his arms flailed about, and his speech was quite slurred. He shared some thoughts about his disability: "If someone sees only my disability, then we can only have an 'I—It' relationship. But if someone ignores my disability—like handing me a cup of hot coffee as if I could manage it like anyone else—then I'm still not being seen for who I am."

In our competitive society, it is still hard to treat disabled children for who they are. Not too long ago, such children were hidden away. Their disability became a reflection on their parents—as if there were something bad or wrong with the parents. They were failures. They weren't winners with whole or healthy children.

Fortunately, there have been some changes in society's attitudes. Witness the incredible integration of Down's syndrome children in families and communities today.

Children who may be seen as "losers" in our competitive society may have the special gifts to be spiritual "winners." Jean Vanier talks about the mentally disabled singing and dancing at the end of the line, and having a wonderful time. They have an ability to trust others and God in a way that most others do not. These children know they can't make it in life on their own; they trust that God and others will love them and care for them. They can enjoy the precious gift of life for its own sake.

This may sound airy-fairy. It hurts to know that a child will never "make it" in our culture's terms, and will probably always experience rejection and discrimination. But these children do have the spiritual gift of knowing they aren't just their achievements, they aren't just their looks, they aren't just their possessions. They are God's beloved children— something most of us take a lifetime to learn.

I see this spiritual gift in a Down's syndrome young man who rides the bus I often take. He's not always well groomed, he's on his way to a "menial" job, but he knows he's somebody. He confidently greets everyone on the bus, making us

feel like somebodies even if we too aren't making it in
society's terms.

What if our children *can* win the competition?

We are naturally proud of children who get top marks at
school, win the prize at the music festival, come first in an
athletic competition. And of course we should celebrate with
our children when they do their best. But being best offers
many temptations for Christians.

A child who does well academically and is rewarded for it
could be tempted to feel superior to a mentally disabled
cousin, or to a classmate everyone considers an "airhead."
Parents have a special responsibility to help this bright child
understand that God loves all children and does not rate one
child as better or more deserving than others because of that
child's particular abilities or blessings.

For example, whenever my children and I were approached
by a dishevelled beggar on the street corner, I always responded with politeness, acknowledging his humanity. I
hoped I was conveying an important message—this person
too deserves respect. If we talk to the minister, the doctor, the
garbage collector, the chimney sweeper, and the mentally
disabled child in the same way, our children know that we
rate them all as our equals.

And children do recognize our attitudes, somehow. A
friend who lived out west for a while ruefully recalls the way
her two-year-old daughter used to act out the exact opposite
of her feelings. When she met the local doctor, a pillar of
church and community, the daughter hid behind her skirts.
When she distastefully avoided a drunk holding up a lamp-
post, the daughter wrapped her arms around his knees!

Children who are winners have a hidden handicap. In our
competitive society, they may accept uncritically the systems
that reward them. Christian people need to help their children
critique any system that values the first and devalues the last.

Maybe a son comes home from first semester at university

saying, "I'm disgusted with David. He got great marks. He got a scholarship into architecture with me. And now he wants to switch to geriatric social work since his grandmother died. Yuck! Why would he want to work with sick old people? He'll never make any money." You might ask him, "Why do you and society consider a career in architecture better than one in geriatric social work? Why do you find work with sick or old people disgusting? Why do social workers who work with sick and old people get less money than architects? Has David discovered that this is where his true talent lies?"

"Winning" children can be seduced into believing they can make it on their own without help. From others. Or from God. Or they might think that only they can do certain tasks, and the outcome depends on them alone. For example, at school they may find it difficult to work on group projects if they think the other group members aren't as talented or as able to produce top-notch results. We parents need to help such children know that we are all part of the body of Christ, of a community of faith, of a people of God. We need the gifts of *everyone* and we need each other's support.

We are not alone. The community is in communion with God as we work together—not competitively—to bring love and justice for all. Not everything depends on us and our ability to "win" and "succeed."

CHAPTER THREE

Sexuality, self-esteem, and the Song of Songs

by Donna Sinclair

When our boys were little, they had ample opportunity to observe the differences between their anatomy and their mother's, in the less-than-private atmosphere of a canoe trip. They commented:

> **Andy:** *Mommy. You no got a penis.*
> **David:** *'Course not. Ladies don't have one.*
> **Andy:** *(comfortingly) You gonna grow one, Mommy. Sometime.*

And I remember when our daughter, Tracy, was similarly sorting out differences, and was astonished by magazine reports about the mother in South Africa who had—literally—carried her daughter's children for her. The grandchildren, triplets, had been inserted in her womb as embryos after the in-vitro fertilization of her daughter's ova with her son-in-

law's sperm. Tracy lay in the tub one evening, having her bath, and carried on a detailed conversation with me about the procedure, growing more and more astounded. Finally she looked up at me, after contemplating her own eight-year-old body smothered in suds. "Girls," she said thoughtfully, "are so much more interesting than boys."

Nothing disconcerts parents more than their children's sexuality. Most modern parents can handle their young one's first questions about "Where did I come from?" with complete composure. But they don't handle quite as well their concerns about junior spending his time in the girls' corner of the kindergarten playing dress-up with women's high heels. And very few can deal comfortably with the left-over condom wrapper found in the 17-year-old's jeans, tossed down the laundry chute. (One moral to draw from this is that children at 17 should be doing their own washing.)

This is partly because we don't always have it all together about our own sexuality. Oh, we have a pretty good idea of our own orientation. Most of us know, by the time we are parents, whether we are heterosexual or homosexual. And we probably know roughly where we stand on such issues as inclusive language and sexism. We may be for or against God being spoken about in strictly male terminology, or in language that includes women as members of the human family, and we may be for or against equal pay for equal work.

But more difficult issues—whether or not homosexual people are also made in the image of God, for example, and whether or not sexual activity is for pleasure, procreation or both, and whether or not my daughter should sleep with her boyfriend—those are a little harder to think through. But think them through we must, or we may find ourselves wounded and afraid when our adolescent children begin to discover themselves as desirable, physical and independent persons. For inevitably, they will discover the possibility of becoming sexually active.

Healthy sexuality starts with self-esteem

The most important gift your children can receive from you, in sexuality as in other areas, is self-esteem. It begins when children are infants, when their first cries of distress are answered and they are picked up, cuddled, fed, comforted. That teaches them that they are worth picking up, worth caring for.

That development of self-esteem continues when the child becomes a toddler, and the toddler's thousands of questions are responded to courteously (or, at least, postponed with the explanation that Mom or Dad is exhausted with all those questions and could-we-have-a-little-break-now-please). It continues when the three-year-old's drawings are proudly taped to the fridge door, when the five-year-old's first attempts at cooking are bravely swallowed, and when the seven-year-old's recitation of the day's events at school is considered as important at the dinner table as the adults' days at work.

Parents continue to nurture their child's self-esteem when the child is pre-adolescent, and (for instance) the declaration that "I am not going to go to church any more" is greeted with respect and careful discussion.

All this care comes to fruition in the adolescent. The moment at a party when the pressure is on to sleep with someone is the moment when the child needs every ounce of self-esteem you have managed to impart.

If the child has always been treated with respect, the child will treat others with respect, and, in turn, demand respect from others. That means that, say, an adolescent girl in this situation, despite the pressures of her friends, has a choice. She may say "No, I don't have to do this. I am my own person, and I know who I am." And the young man may be able to recognize and respect another's autonomy in this situation. (Those roles could be reversed, of course. And their decision could also be a thoughtful "I am my own person, and I'm saying yes.")

It's not simple. But that's a start.

This choice in the bedroom at the party is an important decision. It's going to have to be made by the majority of adolescents, and it's worth spending some time on. But remember that it doesn't happen in isolation. It happens in the context of the previous 15 or 16 or 17 years of your child's life.

Good models of intimacy and sexuality

Next to self-esteem, the most important factor in your child's ability to make that decision in that bedroom is what the infant, and later the toddler, and later the pre-adolescent, observes at home in family life about sexuality. Responsible sexuality needs to be part of the atmosphere of the household from the child's beginning. Discovering it in adolescence is too late.

This is where parents—married or single—need to get their act together. How does a young child note that sexual activity takes place between two grown-up people? Is it an affectionate hug on the stairs? Is sexuality hidden away in bed? This is not conscious teaching, of course. This is information caught, not taught. You don't explain this to your children, nor, obviously, do you invite them into your bedroom. But children notice with enormous precision everything you model for them—including the way you and your partner conduct yourselves with one another.

Does the child observe that each parent is capable of having affectionate friendships with members of the opposite sex without—very important—ending up in bed? In other words, that affection, and even sexual attraction, do not necessarily have to end in intercourse? Don't think your young children don't observe this. At some level, by intuition as much as by logic, they do.

Most important, does the child observe that equality and respect for one another's wishes and feelings is a crucial component of any healthy sexual relationship?

If they do, it's likely they'll demand the same in their own relationships.

What is healthy sexuality, anyway?

Children need to know that companionship and friendship and vulnerability to one another and the ability to change are components of any mature intimate relationship. They need to know that sexual activity belongs *within* intimacy. Sexual activity is not all of intimacy; nor is it a necessary component of an intimate relationship, otherwise we'd never have an intimate relationship with our mother or our father or our Aunt Sarah. But it works best in the kind of mutual openness and trust that *is* the intimate relationship.

Again, children usually do not consciously absorb all this, but—to the extent it is present in your family—it will be absorbed unconsciously over the years of their childhood.

All of this is a big order. In summary, your task, if you want your child to be sexually responsible, is to be sexually responsible yourself. That means expecting love and mutual vulnerability in your *own* sexual relationship with your partner.

But let's go back to the bedroom at the party. Let's assume you have succeeded in endowing your offspring, male or female, with self-esteem, the ability to say "No," and a clear model of what a loving relationship is. So they won't settle for anything less.

They still may end up in bed with someone at the party.

There are several reasons for this. One is that they may indeed be full of self-esteem, and have an ability to say "No," firmly. They may know that sexual intimacy should take place within a mutually loving relationship. However, they may indeed love each other. In a mature way, they may have decided to risk a relationship, both physical and emotional. Some teenagers are more mature than some 40-year-olds.

There is also the whole question of an adolescent's search for identity. Part of that development, as I said in Chapter

One, is to become separate from you. That's an entirely necessary development if children are to become whole human beings. The whole exercise of growing up is about becoming separate from you—or do you want them at home messing up the bathroom *forever*?

But in the process of declaring that separateness, they may reject some of your values, at least for a time. That's why they sometimes decide to be atheists and not go to church. Going to church may be one of your most cherished values. Another value of yours that they may reject is that sex takes place only within marriage.

They will probably try to spare you some of the surprise and even pain of this declaration simply by not letting you know about it. On the other hand, the condom wrapper in the jeans pocket that falls down the laundry chute may not be en- tirely accidental.

Then how are you to feel?

Your first feeling may be betrayal. Or anger. Or even a desire to stick your head in the Cuisinart.

Try to remember that God gave us this difficult and won- derful gift of sexuality, and God is not going to desert our family as we struggle for the wisest way to use it. As a United Church report on human sexuality points out, it is "gift, dilemma and promise." None of us is born wise, and we make mistakes along the way—especially as we begin to grasp our freedom from the family, and our essential separation from our parents. Parents can feel the same kind of pain—and understanding—God must have felt when Adam and Eve decided to go for knowledge and independence instead of comfort and unthinking obedience.

Moving away from the parent hurts. But without it, there's no narrative of humankind, no exodus, no journey, no life.

So you are not necessarily to blame if your 16-year-old daughter or son decides to sleep with someone. It does not make you an unfit mother or father. (Unless, of course, you really did abuse them or set them a terrible example. But if you did, you're probably not going to worry about your son's or daughter's sex experiences, anyway.) It did not happen because you worked too hard when your children were little, or because they are (perhaps) adopted, or because your church failed to instill "proper morals" in them.

This *may* have happened because our society pushes sex in TV commercials and movies.

And it *may* have happened because your child genuinely—perhaps mistakenly—feels ready for this.

But try not to let it happen because your children have such low self-esteem they let someone else decide what's best for them, or because they are grasping for affection they don't get at home.

Of course, all this may be a little beside the point. It may be that you are quite comfortable, as a parent, with your children being sexually active. However, if you aren't, be honest with them. They will have learned to respect your feelings if you respect theirs.

But be respectful, too. This is their territory. It *is* a gift as well as a dilemma. Don't take the gift away from them while you struggle with the dilemma. More than anything, Christianity teaches us about grace, both for our children and ourselves. God has more to worry about than two people trying to find out what it is to be in love. And God has a lot of patience with parents and children struggling to find out how to get along.

Education about safe sex

We are almost ready to leave that bedroom at the party. Except for one more thing. We still need to educate them about the hazards of sex. This is not easy. Even the most liberal of us don't want to be thought of as encouraging our children to have sex.

Furthermore, as they become teenagers, they need privacy. How would you like to have had the shadow of your parents present at your first kiss? Much of this they must figure out for themselves. The fact that you are their parent excludes you from the process, except by way of preparation, which is what you have been about for the past 15 or 16 years.

Unless you have an unusually open household, mostly you need to get out of the way and hope that you have done reasonably well.

Still, there are some things you *can* do. You can keep an eye on the sex education classes in your local school. They may form the basis for useful dinner-table discussion. And if these classes are well done, they offer your children what you can't—discussion about sexual mores with a respected adult other than their parents. With their peers present, there is a better understanding in their own subculture of what's a good idea and what isn't. If the classes are not well handled—meaning they either separate sex from intimacy, or are so awkwardly taught that no one gets anything out of it—you can quietly try to influence the school to do a better job.

You can make sure that material that will educate them is lying around the house. Most major magazines in the last few years have carried cover stories on AIDS, for instance. It's hard to miss the reality of this problem when it is emblazoned all over a magazine's cover in living color. If you simply leave the publication on the coffee table, and if your adolescent can read, it will get picked up. Make sure it's a reputable magazine, though. If it's a denominational magazine, which can handle the subject sensitively within the context of your faith, rejoice. It may give them an increased understanding of their faith along with the information they need. But a word of caution—do not hand them the magazine and say "Here, read this," or even, "You would really like this!" Let them find it on their own.

You can also talk about sexual hazards, including unwanted pregnancies, when and if the opportunity arises. Being judgmental will, of course, get you nowhere. Keep an open mind. You may learn something too. Some teens know more about sexually transmitted diseases than you do. More important, you may be relieved to discover that your son *does* know he is financially responsible for any children he may father, until those children are 18. (If he doesn't know this, tell him. Gently. If his eyebrows go up and his Adam's apple bobs furiously, try not to demand why he's worried.)

Encouraging your adolescents to baby-sit, or work as lifeguards or playground supervisors, may be good reality therapy. Cuddly, sweet babies grow up to be exuberant children, and they are with you for a long, long time. Once adolescents understand that, they may abstain or act responsibly in a way that lectures from you could never accomplish.

But be careful with scare tactics. Yes, you have to be clear with them that sexuality is a dilemma. But don't take away the gift and the promise that it contains. They may never get it back.

Finally, choose your family physician with care. If your daughter or son decides, without your knowledge, to be sexually active, it's good to have a family doctor whom your child trusts, with whom your child can discuss birth control.

Aren't Christians supposed to be virgins when they marry?

We wish we had a rule to give you about that. We wish we could say clearly that it is either absolutely right or forbidden to have sexual relations without a marriage certificate, even if both partners are 50 years old and holding down responsible jobs. Unfortunately, scripture isn't always clear about these things. Nor is life. We may have to do some thinking for ourselves about these matters.

One thing *is* clear, though. From our reading of scripture (for example, the Magnificat in Luke 1:46–55) we know that God doesn't like oppression and injustice. People who find themselves in a sexual relationship in which they are being exploited, where the relationship is not equal, are not in a relationship we could call "Christian." Most teenagers don't yet have a clear enough sense of self to be anything but vulnerable in a sexual relationship. They are terribly open to being exploited; that's one reason we usually disapprove of teenage sex.

The other reason is harder to define. It has something to do with an understanding most Christians don't have clear in our heads yet: our bodies are gifts from God and God delights in our sexuality. God celebrates all the wonderful sensual delight that is inherent in the Song of Songs, of which we are still a little suspicious.

We believe—and wish we could convey to all youth—that our bodies are to be loved profoundly. That means that they are not for giving away lightly, but only with the kind of joy that comes with absolute trust and vulnerability. It takes a while to find someone you can trust like that.

All these things are very hard to think through and discuss with your child. But they are not nearly as hard as discovering that your adolescent has AIDS, or that you are going to be a grandparent unexpectedly early, or simply that something very precious—your child's sexuality—has been abused.

Your child and sexual abuse

That leads into a discussion of another difficult topic: how do we protect our children, of any age, from being sexually abused?

Re-read the beginning of this chapter—read it seriously. The key word in protecting your child from sexual abuse is *self-esteem*. To be safe, your child needs the ability to say "No" to an adult, even one who is in authority. Your child needs an informed sense of self: "I know I am a worthy human being who has inalienable rights, and one of those rights is to the integrity of my own body." Your children also need to be able to trust you, the parent, to hear seriously whatever they say. Even if it is something you don't want to hear. Like what a trusted person—a babysitter, a teacher, a relative—may have tried to do with them.

That means we have to re-think a basic parental concept:

unquestioning obedience. It would be nice, and certainly easier to be parents, if our children obeyed all our commands like little robots. I would not, for instance, be sitting here typing while wondering if the vacuuming and dishes I assigned this morning were getting done. But as we are discovering today, obeying anyone in authority without questioning can be extraordinarily dangerous. Children need to be able to ask why you consider this or that to be a good thing. Children need the opportunity to weigh your ideas, and get their point across.

Unquestioning obedience is a concept we have already had to re-think in terms of our theology. Most of us no longer believe in a strict Father-God, who prefers males to serve him, uses images for the church like "marching as to war," and eventually hopes to triumphantly conquer the whole world. Many of us are moving closer and closer to an understanding of a God who nurtures us, who yearns for us to be in relationship with God, who comes into the world in a human body, as a little child. This God mourns with us when we are sad, dances with us when we are happy, needs us, and longs to give us power, not deprive us of it.

The blunt fact is that if we believe in the latter kind of God, and raise our children accordingly, they are far less likely to be vulnerable to those who need to have power over someone before they can express themselves sexually—in other words, sexual abusers. Again, our vision of God affects the way we raise our children.

And of course, the less society in general believes in a harsh macho God who has absolute authority to control everyone, the fewer men—we hope—will model themselves after "Him." It's important to remember that most sexual abuse is inflicted by someone the child knows—and far too often it is the father. That activity is frequently fuelled by a terrible and false belief that men are divinely ordained to be dominant and that inequality of power is a prerequisite for sex.

All this may mean that we have to sit and think over the
questions:
- What do I believe about God?
- How am I to be with this child?
- What is the model God holds up for me as a parent?

We may have to think about such questions over and over
through the years, as we try to figure out this delicate and
changeable task of child-rearing.

Allowing children to question you doesn't mean you need to be a doormat

We are called to be parents, not slaves. But we do need to
give our children room to think for themselves. That is, after
all, what God gives us. It's called free will. I can marshal all
sorts of reasons why my children should do the vacuuming
and dish washing, including the consequences of having a
hurt, angry, and uncooperative mother because she was left
with the household chores when she had a deadline.

But having a sense of *self*-worth also helps us recognize
another's worth. I am a worthwhile "other" to my children—
and so the vacuuming gets done.

Children need to know they *can* question, and that they are
worthy. And they need to know it from a very early age.
None of that self-trust and self-esteem is going to miracu-
lously appear the moment a stranger puts his hand on your
daughter's thigh in a darkened theatre, or a doctor or minister
or teacher touches your child in inappropriate ways. That
sense of self-worth has to be ingrained, instinctive, practiced
on your children from the beginning.

Self-esteem also comes from being listened to, in conversations around the dinner table. Forget the old maxim, "Children are to be seen and not heard." Children who are *not* heard
are vulnerable. Self-esteem comes from being allowed from
an early age to make whatever decisions one is capable of—
especially those which concern the integrity of one's own
body. So children choose what they are going to wear, for

example. If it is cold and they choose to wear shorts, let them discover for themselves how uncomfortable "taking the consequences" can be.

Of course, taking the consequences of their actions has to be tempered with common sense. The consequences of playing with matches and crossing the street without looking are cases in point. But allowing young children to decide how they will act in matters affecting primarily themselves is good preparation for the day they will have to decide whether or not to take the consequences of not studying, or of living entirely on junk food, or of hanging out with the drug dealers at the wrong end of the school.

In other words, you are developing their capacity for independent thought. It helps if children know that the parent will back them up emotionally, of course. But that won't relieve them of the consequences of their action. Or inaction. For example:

Sam: (age 10): I didn't do very well on my math.

Mother: That must make you feel bad.

Sam: Yeah. I don't like that teacher much. That's why I didn't study.

Mother: Sometimes we don't like the people who have some power over us.

Sam: I sure don't like her.

Mother: Any way I can help? I'm sorry I'm not better in math myself—I sure can't help you study!

Sam: Could you phone the teacher and tell her I was sick that day?

Mother: You've got to be kidding.

Sam: (grinning) Just thought I'd try.

Mother: (without being judgmental or accusing) Do you have any other ideas?

Sam: Well, could you keep the house quiet tomorrow night, and keep Susie from having all her little friends over and running around and screaming? I've got another math test.

Mother: Sure. Susie's old enough to respect study times.

The sequel to that story, we hope, is that Sam will do better on the next test. But more than that, he'll have an improved sense of his own worth. Mother did not step in to save him from the consequences of his inaction. On the other hand, mother was there, and calm. So Sam knows there will be no overreaction, no matter what he has to say. This is important for the next scenario, which goes as follows:

Sam: I'm going to quit soccer.

Mother: I'm surprised—I thought you really liked it.

Sam: I do.

Mother: (Silence, waiting.)

Sam: (Slightly embarrassed) The coach is always patting my bum.

Mother: (Now all ears, and trying to keep her voice even.) Oh?

Sam: He does it to the other kids too. It makes me feel funny.

Mother: Yes. It would make me feel funny too. Do you think he does it 'cause he thinks that's part of being a jock, or what?

Sam: I don't know.

Mother: Do you *want* to quit soccer?

Sam: No. I really do like it. I could tell him how much it bothers me.

Mother: That's a good idea. Let's talk to Dad about it too. If that doesn't work, we'll all go and see the coach together, if that's okay with you.

Sam: Are you upset?

Mother: Yes, and confused. But I think we need to deal with this. I'm glad you told me.

Sam: You won't make a big fuss about it?

Mother: I know you don't want to be embarrassed. You talk to him first. And then if we have to, I think we can talk about this quietly. But we also want to know if other kids are really upset too, but don't feel they can say anything.

Of course, that's a pretty mild scenario. In other cases, parents might need to be more alert, as in this excerpt from *Am I the Only One?* (Douglas & McIntyre). It's a collection by Dennis Foon and Brenda Knight of stories by children who have been abused.

Rebecca

"I am a twelve-year-old girl in grade seven. Somebody abused me. He really hurt me and made my life miserable. His name was Ralph. He was my babysitter and a friend of my mother's but in real life he was mean. He was supposed to be a friend to me but that's not what he turned out to be.

"I think I was six or seven when it happened. He was sixteen or seventeen. These things happened when he came over and babysat which was usually once or twice a week. I think it happened about seven times.

"When it was happening it felt really bad. He was really heavy, and at six or seven, I wasn't very big so it really hurt. Most of my body from the waist down really hurt. I had asked him to stop but he wouldn't...

"I thought it was normal... Everybody says go and tell your parents. But it's really hard for someone to do. I didn't tell because I didn't want to get the reaction of my mother's and father's faces hurt. I really didn't want to hurt them. I thought they would really be sad that it happened to me, and that they would be really mad at Ralph—which is what I wanted them to be—but I couldn't say it."

We can't protect our children completely from the world. But we can reduce the possibility of abuse happening, and continuing. Rebecca, for example, needed some vocabulary with which to explain what was going on. (One expert on child abuse suggests that parents who have difficulty using words like "penis" and "vagina" with their children practice such words aloud under the noise of vacuuming or mowing lawn.) There is also an assortment of picture books for very young children, who are not exempt from abuse, that will provide them and their parents with the language they need.

Rebecca also needed to feel that her parents could handle what had been going on. She did eventually manage to tell them. Her mother was indeed "really, really sad, like I expected her to be." But her father phoned the police, protecting other children from the ministrations of this sitter. And her mother took her to the family doctor. "I thought I was broken from the inside," she explains, "...but the doctor said, 'No, you're okay.'"

The book is filled with painfully true stories like that one. This does happen, far too often. No child can be completely shielded from these harsh possibilities, however, and we do our children a disservice if we overprotect them, or frighten them away from the sheer joy of cuddling into a loving grandparent's lap, for example. There is evil in the world. As Christians, we recognize that.

What we *can* do is give them some tools to help them deal with the possibility of exploitation and abuse. We can fill them with the sense that they are God's creatures, precious and unique; we can assure them that we love them unconditionally, in the way God loves us; we can model respectful behavior around their friends—never, for instance, picking up a small child without asking permission from that child first.

Then we can hope for the courage and compassion that flows from a belief in a gentle and loving and nurturing God.

And what if your child is gay?

One good thing about the culture we live in is that it is becoming easier to talk about sexual orientations. Some people are homosexual, and some are heterosexual. The difficult thing is that—despite Jesus' example of inclusiveness—many people find it hard to accept those they feel to be different from themselves. This gets especially awkward when it involves your own child.

> She is a mature woman who spends quite a lot of her time going to various groups talking about homosexuality. She is well qualified to do that. A lesbian herself, she knows the gay world well. I sat and watched her fielding questions from a group of attentive church people, intent on defining their own attitudes toward people who express their sexuality in this way. Someone wondered what advice she would give to a young person who felt he or she was homosexual.
>
> "Don't tell your parents," she said bluntly, to the obvious surprise of most of her audience. "What usually happens, when an adolescent (especially a boy) tells a parent (especially Dad) about this, is that the adolescent is immediately kicked out of the house.'You can leave...you're no son of mine...'"
>
> It wasn't pleasant listening.

As a Christian parent, you can make sure that your child never hears those words: "You can leave..." He or she *could* turn out to be homosexual—roughly ten percent of the world's population is. But he or she is still, unalterably, the child you love. If you are worried about your six-year-old, gentle son playing dress-up with the girls' clothes at play school, or your six-year-old girl playing hockey (neither, by the way, indications of homosexuality) it might be good for you to do some thinking now about where you stand.

Here are some facts to ponder:

1. As far as social science knows right now, sexual orientation for most people seems to be not a choice

but a given. Theorists have investigated a lot of possible factors in determining sexual preference, but nobody really knows for sure what makes someone heterosexual or homosexual.

2. One fairly certain thing is that we exist on a continuum of sexual preference. According to Alfred Kinsey's research, which has been added to but not significantly challenged over the last 30 years, about 14% of males and about 7% of females are exclusively homosexual. About 61% of both are exclusively heterosexual. Everyone else, somewhere along the continuum Kinsey proposed, has some bisexual *preferences*, though not necessarily behavior. (In other words, these people might live in faithful, monogamous partnerships all through their adult life.)

3. Some people declare they have been "healed" of their homosexuality, although it is not considered a disease, and it's not catching. Many others have accepted who they are, have struggled to come "out of the closet" and leave behind the stress of hiding their identity. They would like to live as Christians in loving, faithful relationships within a faith community. Unfortunately, as one gay person says, "Sometimes the stress of 'coming out' can be a lot worse than hiding it."

4. Most gay people are not—despite popular stereotypes—promiscuous. A study by Bell and Weinberg, for example, "Homosexualities, a Study of Diversity Among Men and Women" [cited in George Edwards: *Gay/Lesbian Liberation: A Biblical Perspective* (Pilgrim Press)] concludes that "relatively few homosexuals conform to the stereotype."

There is much more to know about homosexuality, and much has been written on the subject. But your question as a parent is "What if...?" How would you handle it? What would you do? It's good to think these questions through, because your child would benefit from your support. Homosexual people still have a hard road to follow. Only three provinces—Ontario, Quebec and Manitoba—have legislation prohibiting discrimination on the basis of sexual orientation. Although the federal government has promised to include it in Canada's Charter of Rights and Freedoms, there is some concern (at the time I write this) that such legislation will be delayed because of the furor over Ontario's legislation.

Even where there is such legislation, homosexual people are still hampered in their careers; they still often find it necessary to remain "in the closet," especially if they work in school systems. They still suffer through gay jokes. As one lesbian woman explains, "I still cringe every time I hear them at work. Sometimes I feel my co-workers are testing me, that deep down they know I'm a lesbian, and want to see what I'll say."

And—as in the anecdote earlier in this section—they are sometimes profoundly cut off from their families.

So what would I do if...?

What if your child does come to you and say, "I'm gay"? How would you handle that? We asked some gay people—including a minister—for advice.

- *Accept that you may have grieving to do.* "This is not unlike the process one goes through with any significant loss," says one minister who is homosexual. "There is the initial shock, denial, anger and—hopefully at some time—acceptance."

  You will have lost a potential son- or daughter-in-law, and, if this is your only child, probably the chance to babble proudly about grandchildren. This is a very real and important loss.

• *Accept that you may now live with some new worries.* "Many parents of homosexual people," this minister explains, "react with a very real fear for their children's safety and happiness. 'Queer bashing' and job loss are a reality for most gay and lesbian people. They may have to live with the dread that their child will be the victim of some bigot's violence."

• *Know that all this is not because of your action or inaction.* Once again, despite much study, there is no clear evidence about exactly what makes a person homosexual or heterosexual. But studies by Bell and Weinberg and others indicate that all the old theories, which included "rejecting" mothers and "passive" fathers, have little value. At the moment, it seems quite unlikely that your child's orientation is affected by something you did or didn't do.

Even children who are abused don't necessarily respond by turning away from all those who are the same sex as the abuser. According to Ellen Bass and Laura Davis, authors of *The Courage to Heal* (Harper & Row) an important book for survivors of child sexual abuse, "no one becomes a lesbian solely because she was abused by a man... If abuse were the determining factor in sexual preference, the lesbian population would be far greater than it is now..."

• *Make sure you have support while you work this through*, just as you would if you were confronted with any significant grief situation. Find a sympathetic third person (one who knows something about sexual orientation) who can help you talk through your feelings about your child's orientation, both alone and in the presence of your child. Many religious denominations have associations of gay people within them, and many parents have joined those associations for both support and information.

• *Do some very thoughtful Bible study.* Many Christians, we think mistakenly, have accepted a reading of the Bible that says homosexuality is wrong. They point to the holiness code in Leviticus, for example. You might try re-thinking that code in the light of Jesus' teachings. He very clearly challenges that code, referring to those who abide by it slavishly as "whited sepulchres," at the same time as he displays great compassion for the outcasts of society. Above all, we can gather from Jesus' teachings that being holy is not about having a certain orientation. It's about being more loving.

• *Work for change.* As the parent of any child, we are called to work for the kind of world where everyone is accepted. We can do that, not just as parents, but as Christians. The Christian church feels strongly the Gospel imperative to justice. We don't like to see anyone as victim: not refugees, not people who live in poverty, not the approximately 10% of human beings all over the world who are sexually attracted to people of the same sex.

There's another reason why we, especially as Christian parents, need to work for change. The Christian Church itself has some history that needs healing. Even though Jesus modeled a behavior of inclusion, some churches have used those biblical passages as reason for condemning homosexual people. These churches trumpet an "I told you so" message of vengeance on people who have AIDS, although the disease affects heterosexual as well as homosexual people. They ignore the extreme unlikelihood that the God who loved us enough to live—and die—as one of us would punish us for an orientation that doesn't seem a matter of choice.

A note about sex roles

All of these concepts are easier if you as a parent can escape from the kind of stereotyping that suggests little girls should wear dresses, play with dolls, and be calm and quiet, while little boys play hockey, play with guns, and are aggressive.

Those stereotypes are dissipating, as they should. A careful reading of scripture shows Jesus treating women as equals. But stereotypes still exist. As I write this, governments continue to debate funding of universal day care. Some still believe, apparently, that there is only one possible shape for the *real* family: Dad at work and Mom at home caring for the children.

There is much written about this topic. I'm not going to repeat it, except to suggest that part of surviving the sexual turbulence of adolescence is to help your children know that girls are not passive "yes-people" and boys are not aggressive competitors, in and out of the bedroom. That may sound overstated. It's not.

On their own

Sexuality is one area of our children's lives where we will not be present with them—at least, not physically. And yet, as I said at the beginning, our own sexuality will be with them, as a model to accept or to reject. Whether or not we model an easy intimacy and graceful affection and comfort with our own bodies and love for our partner, our children will intuit our attitudes about our bodies and hearts.

What follows then, is a kind of creed. It's what we happen to believe about sexuality and God. You might want to sit down and make up your own creed, as your way of expressing what you want your children to see in you:

- We believe that God calls us into intimate relationship with others, and models this in affection and yearning for us.
- We believe that God worries less about the *rules* of

sexual relationships (you shall not sleep with anyone before you are married to them) than about the
quality of them (you shall not be exploitive; you
shall not take advantage of the vulnerability and
need for affection of someone less strong than you;
above all, you shall not—ever—be abusive or cruel
in any way).

To put it another way: content (what goes on in
relationships) and form (the institutionalized shape
of relationships—like marriage) are not separate.
The form is important, but it does not automatically
make a relationship just.

- We believe that affection and mutual attraction can
exist between two people without that affection cul-
minating in a sexual relationship. In other words,
two single people, or two people married to others,
can be friends.

- We believe marriage is sexually exclusive. If you
can't model that for your children, you may right-
fully expect their wrath, disappointment, and an-
guish. They are, after all, the fruit and symbol of the
covenant you made at your wedding—a covenant
between God, your spouse and you—to be faithful
to one another.

- We believe, on the other hand, that grace abounds.
Marriages may be torn, promises broken. Sometimes they can be mended. Sometimes not. But God
continues to love us in our imperfection.

- Above all, we believe our sexuality is a gift and
offering to God, an expression of delight in the
universe God made, and a celebration. We cannot
separate our "body" selves from our "spiritual"
selves. We are whole human beings. Our bodies and
minds and spirits interact. And God delights in that
knowledge with us.

CHAPTER FOUR

Conflict, courage, and self-defense

by Yvonne Stewart

I often sit on my front porch on summer weekends and watch neighbors "relaxing." In one family the parents and other adults sit around a table in their side yard drinking bottles of beer while their two children noisily and energetically ride their bikes around them.

Frequently the children call out "Mum! Mum! Mum!"

Mother irritably bawls out "What?" They demonstrate their newest bike-riding trick.

After several such exchanges, mother shouts, "Stop bugging me or I'll punch you in the face!" The stepfather gets up and moves toward the children to try to do just that. The children slink off to a nearby parkette, where I soon see them shouting at their playmates, punching and kicking them.

I also remember when a friend's sons fought so viciously that one brother actually tried to hang the other.

Such incidents sadden me. I wish life could be nicer for these children and free from such harsh conflicts and confrontations.

But then I also think of children who have had a "nicer" life—who have been taught to be polite, well-mannered, and cooperative, taught to avoid conflict and fighting. These children never openly disagree with adults or other children. But when the tension of conflict arises in them, instead of punching or kicking, they wait for "the teacher's back to be turned" and then indulge in ugly face-making and rude name calling.

Is that really any better? Does either kind of child grow up to be the kind of person who will—in small or big ways—reduce tensions in our world?

Christian parents today are challenged to think about how to raise children so that they can deal with conflict in ways that won't make them either "Rambos" or back-stabbers.

Conflict is part of life

To begin with, we need to acknowledge that conflict is a natural part of life. It needs to be dealt with in constructive ways. Sometimes it's tempting to think that if we don't give our children war toys and if we make sure they don't watch violent TV programs, and if we only let them play cooperative games, we will protect them from conflict. But conflict can't be avoided. People will always have different needs and expectations in life and different points of view.

The best we parents can do is help our children cope with conflict in healthy and creative ways that enhance life and bring peace with justice rather than destroy life and all creation.

Keeping up appearances vs. recognizing conflict

Openly admitting to disagreements and conflicts in everyday life isn't always easy for middle-class and Christian families. Our North American society still upholds as its ideal

the stereotype of a "nice happy family" that only has mild
disagreements over such things as allowances and curfews.
Even when television programs show families who have
made it through the intense conflicts of separation and divorce or rebellious adolescence, we still get the impression
that a family in conflict is not a success. And in our society,
who wants to admit to being a failure? So we keep our tensions and differences behind closed doors, or, even better, out
of our consciousness altogether.

The Christian church also puts a lot of emphasis on unity—
one body of Christ, one church, one faith, one baptism and
one peace among all people. And so Christian families may
often feel that they must be unified and cheerful to be faithful.

When a child in a Christian family announces that she
hates her brother, it's tempting to respond, "Of course, you
don't hate him. He's your brother. Sisters love their brothers
in this family."

This response only teaches the child to deny her feelings.
If she keeps pushing down her negative feelings toward her
brother, she may also repress the positive loving ones. Or,
instead of honestly expressing her feelings, she may find
devious ways of venting them—like "accidentally" leaving
his bike behind the family car.

It would be much better for the little girl, and her brother,
if a parent acknowledged the reality of her feelings: "You're
really furious with him, aren't you?" Once the daughter
knows her feelings are accepted, perhaps she can explain why
she feels that way. Such a conversation might lead eventually
to a constructive resolution of conflict.

The Bible acknowledges conflict

Scripture helps us recognize the reality of conflict. The
Bible is full of descriptions of conflicts, among the Hebrew
people and later among the new Christians, and of conflicts
between these peoples and other groups and nations. These
conflicts weren't always resolved constructively either. The

Bible has no pretense that disagreements and conflicts didn't exist.

When the Hebrew slaves cried out because their basic human requirements conflicted with the power-seeking demands of the Egyptians, God responded and escalated the conflict from threats, to plagues, to destruction of life.

When the Hebrew people neglected their part of their covenant with God—by worshipping other gods and treating each other unjustly—God initiated conflict through the prophets. Shape up, said God, in effect, or get shipped out! The Hebrew people would be captured, and sent into exile.

Jesus, too, experienced much conflict:

- internally, over crucial decisions (temptations in the desert)
- with his disciples ("get behind me, Satan!")
- with religious leaders who valued law over love (healing the crippled man on the Sabbath)
- with business interests that valued profit over worship of God (money-changers in the Temple)
- with the upper social classes, over God's intentions ("He sits with sinners and outcasts").

Jesus died because what he stood for—God's kingdom—conflicted with the values of the powerful. He died on the ultimate symbol of conflict, where good and evil "cross."

Even after Jesus' death and resurrection, his disciples, particularly followers of Peter and John, formed conflicting factions. Paul had many arguments with new churches about how they conducted themselves. And the new churches themselves were in conflict with their communities and suffered persecution.

Biblical consequences of conflict

When we look at the consequences people in the Bible suffered for conflict, it's not hard to see why we are reluctant to deal with it. Who wants angry arguments, physical violence, persecution, and death?

On the other hand, we must recall that there are also consequences if we try to avoid conflict, wherever hate and injustice and unfaithfulness contradict God's requirement of love and justice and faithfulness. The consequence is exile—from God and from each other. The promise of the new covenant in Christ is that if we enter into conflict to bring about God's reign of love, God will be with us. New life will come, no matter what the difficulties involved.

Before the Roman emperor, Constantine, converted to Christianity, Christians were tortured and killed because they refused to worship the Roman gods and goddesses and their earthly representative, the emperor. They refused to accept the social hierarchy which rated people according to class, family, gender, wealth, education and status as free person or slave. They refused to pay taxes, which supported the emperor's luxuries. They chose to confront Roman values and live a conflicting lifestyle—worshipping one God, preaching and living as if all people were equal, and voluntarily giving money to the destitute.

Christians lost that commitment to confronting injustice when Constantine made Christianity the official state religion of Rome, in the 4th century.

Once Constantine converted, churches became prominent. And Christians, especially bishops, got tax exemptions, increased income, and social and political power. So church leaders began to change their philosophy. Instead of encouraging people to critique government as in the past, they began to suggest that since all are sinners, people need government (especially if it's Christian) to keep them in line. We've been influenced by this idea of obedience to authority for our own good ever since.

Religion and state are theoretically separate in our society today. In fact, many of us benefit from the state. Some of us work for the state; others get grants and funding; still others get tax breaks. Almost everyone benefits from one government legislation or another. But these systems aren't always equitable or just. Some are always penalized; some always suffer. Because of the benefits we receive, it's not easy to confront those systems for the sake of the people who suffer under them. If things seem peaceful and pleasant for us, why upset the apple cart? Doesn't God want us to have peace and the abundant life? But God wants the abundant life for all. There can be no peace until all have it—until justice is done.

Biblically and historically, God calls Christians to undertake this task of justice-making, of kingdom-bringing—even if it leads us into conflict.

Conflict can be creative

If that principle applies in national and social issues—and I believe it does—it also applies within the family.

While conflict is always risky, it can also be healing and creative. Openly discussing different desires, expectations, points of view—as Jesus did with his disciples, and Paul did with his congregations—can help us develop new understandings and change our ways. My son and I went through a period of constant hassles over the mess he strewed throughout our home. Finally, the tension between us forced us to sit down and talk it out. I explained that since I led such a busy life, going in so many different directions, it meant a lot to me to come home to a space that had some order and comfort to it. Bryan complained that he felt he always had to live by my rules, and he wanted a chance to live his way. We finally compromised. Bryan would keep the common spaces like kitchen, dining room, living room free of his clutter. But I would stay out of his room and let him keep it as he chose—as long as he kept the door closed!

We both came out of this conflict better understanding each other's needs, and more willing to change our behavior for the benefit of both of us. We were able to hang in with each other, listen to each other, and resolve our differences—because we love each other, and were committed to living together as a family.

Dealing with conflict

Some means for dealing with conflict

Christians are called to create or cope with conflict wherever God's will is not being done. So it is part of our responsibility as Christian parents to help our children do this too.

Jesus did not avoid conflict in his life. Matthew reports Jesus saying "I bring not peace but a sword" (Matthew 10:34). Jesus knew that his message of God's kingdom could create conflict. It did. And he dealt with it in a variety of ways:

- He withdrew from the situation after speaking in the synagogue in Nazareth (Luke 4:28–30)
- He avoided it by "not traveling openly in Judea" (John 11:54)
- He confronted injustice by speaking out—calling the Pharisees "whited sepulchres" (Matthew 23:27–28)
- He took the risk of offending others and inciting conflict by acting faithfully—healing on the Sabbath (Luke 6:6–11)
- He built support for himself by attracting followers to his/God's vision and point of view—healing and teaching (Matthew 12:9–13; 13:1–52)
- He turned the other cheek (Luke 6:29)—the capture in Gethsemane (Luke 22:49–51)
- He loved his enemies—forgiving even his executioners (Luke 23:24)

We can, and probably do, practice all of those some of the time. Depending on our personalities, we may prefer some of those tactics more than others. There's no single right way to deal with conflict. After all, even Jesus sometimes simply avoided it.

Jesus also taught his disciples to be "wise as serpents and gentle as doves" (Matthew 10:16) in conflict situations. We parents need to pass on this wisdom to our children so that they can learn to deal with conflict constructively and creatively.

Here's a story of a girl—I'll call her Judy—who had acquired some of this wisdom by the early age of seven. One day at school, a child left the classroom without asking permission. The teacher vehemently chastised the whole class for disobedience, and denied them all privileges. On her way home at lunchtime, Judy marched up to the teacher's desk and said bravely, "You aren't being very nice. We don't deserve to be treated this way. We haven't done anything to you."

The teacher was simply having a bad day. She saw Judy's point and was able to make amends with the class. But Judy took a risk. She could have made things worse. She could have been labeled a troublemaker, and been punished for the slightest infraction of rules from then on. In spite of this possibility, the child had enough self-esteem to know that she and her classmates didn't deserve the criticism and punishment they had received. She had learned at home to express her point of view; she was confident that it would be heard. And she had a combination of courage and intuition (as to how far she could go) that enabled her to confront the teacher's unjust act.

We parents usually don't want our children to be seen as troublemakers. We want people in authority, such as teachers, to think we have nice children. And we certainly don't want our children to suffer any unnecessary punishment. Our inclination is to encourage them to avoid conflict or "trouble" and mind their own business. But as Christians, are we supposed to mind our own business? Or to mind *God's* business?

Acknowledge our differences

The first step in dealing with conflict is acknowledging its existence. But we can't stop there.

As a second step, we need to take a good look at what's causing the conflict. Sometimes disagreements between people arise not because their respective needs and rights clash, but because they don't understand or accept each other's point of view and abilities. Paul talks about the different gifts in the body of Christ—teaching, preaching, healing, speaking in tongues and so on. He tried to encourage the early Christians to appreciate each other's gifts and their contribution to the work of the church rather than arguing over the relative values of each.

We need to do this in our families in our daily lives. I have a gift for being organized and for meeting deadlines. My children don't. I had to work very hard—I don't think I ever quite succeeded—at accepting that my children work much better under last-minute pressure. Personally, I would fall apart. It was hard for me to learn to keep my mouth shut and not to nag them constantly to "hurry up." Nagging incited some very tense conflict.

There are many books around about right brain and left brain thinkers, about the Myers-Briggs personality profiles, about different styles of learning and different stages of intellectual, faith and moral development. Some parents might find it interesting and helpful to read them. But the most important thing to remember is that our children have different talents and gifts, different ways of thinking and learning, than we do, than their friends do. Accepting this at home, and helping our children accept this in other relationships, can go a long way to preventing unnecessary conflict.

Let them work it out on their own

Sometimes people can't accept these differences, and conflict does result. Angry shouts or fisticuffs often announce conflict among our children. "She hit me first!" screams one. "He's lying," asserts another. Then comes an appeal to us to take sides, to settle things for them.

Sometimes the best thing to do is to refuse, to back off and leave them to fight it out. Nancy, two years older than Bryan, used to get extremely frustrated with me when I wouldn't

defend her from Bryan's reported assaults. (Don't we sometimes feel that way about God? Why isn't God here taking
our side?) I simply said that I didn't see the start of the fight,
so I *couldn't* take her side. And anyway, I had confidence that
she could work it out. (Doesn't God too have the confidence
that we can work things out—if we follow the way of love?)

In time, she began to believe in her own ability to deal with
her brother. She learned to use her own power to resolve
difficulties rather than trying to escalate the situation by
bringing in more "heavy duty" power on her side. Maybe if
our children learn to trust in their own abilities to resolve
conflict, they might not feel they need weapons to defend
their positions when they grow up.

Model ways of dealing with conflict

Nancy didn't learn to resolve differences solely on her own
through trial and error. Nor will most children. Parents can
help children understand and deal with conflict by the way we
deal with the disagreements between ourselves and them.
Thus we help them to think about fights they have with
siblings and friends and to apply new ways of behaving in
these situations.

Taking your child's side against a friend, regardless, may
demonstrate family loyalty. But so does the Mafia. You've
modeled one way of dealing with conflict.

Refusing to get involved at all models another way of
dealing with conflict.

Taking the time to talk things out models a third way. If
you've read this far in the book, you'll know it's our pre-
ferred choice.

Learn about the dynamics of conflict

If we and our children understand the dynamics of conflict,
we can prevent it. Or, sometimes, we can avoid escalating the
conflict. By recognizing what's happening, we can come up
with ways of resolving the conflict.

Usually conflict originates in a *fear* that a wish or want or expectation will not be met. Remember the mother in the story at the beginning of this chapter? She was probably afraid that her wish for companionship with her husband and friends would be disturbed when her children called to her. Or that she couldn't be one of the group. Peer pressure, in an adult context. (The religious leaders of Jesus' time were similarly afraid that Jesus' popularity with the people would jeopardize their own power and influence.)

To cope with their fear that the "nasty other side" won't allow their expectation to be fulfilled, people adapt one of these defenses:
- fighting, determined they will win
- fighting, convinced they will lose
- acknowledging fear and conflict, but avoiding dealing with it
- repressing the fear and denying there is any conflict at all.

Which defensive behavior did the mother use?

We need to help our children, in conflict, to identify their feelings and wishes, and to see the other person's point of view. That's a form of loving your enemy—trying to see the situation through their eyes and their emotions. Then it's possible to examine and choose appropriate ways to resolve the conflict so the expectations on both sides can be met, or at least acknowledged.

A family case study

A friend of mine—I'll call her Susan—took her youngest daughter, Penny, a bright nine-year-old, shopping with her. While out, they found a shoe store that had a sale on shoes in Penny's size. Since Penny often had a hard time getting reasonably priced shoes that fit, Susan bought her two pairs. They returned home, pleased with themselves and their purchase. But when Penny's older and more easily fitted sister, Helen, discovered the large purchase, she blew up:

"You're mean. You *always* buy things for Penny and never for me."

There was much foot-stamping, throwing of pillows around the room and imprecations directed to her sister: "I hate you! I hate you!" and to her mother "I want something *right now.* You have to make it up to me. You're mean!"

Does that sound at all familiar? Let's look at what's going on here. Identifying feelings is always a good way to start. One thing is obvious in this situation—the elder daughter, Helen, is angry. Angry at her mother for not getting her something. Angry at her sister for getting something. Angry at herself for not going with them so she could get something too.

And there is more going on underneath. Helen is afraid. She is threatened by her bright, attractive and competent younger sister. Any indication that her sister has more than she does makes her fear that her position as senior child might be usurped—a position that she very much wants to keep.

Helen also portrays herself as "in the right"—the hard-done-by victim—while her mother is "wrong" and "mean," and her sister hate-inspiring. While that's natural enough—who's going to start by painting themselves "in the wrong"?—it also makes it very difficult for her to see any point of view other than her own.

Helen's defense was to fight with the intention of winning. By any means. No matter how she made others feel. She nagged, insulted, and carried on until Susan weakened and bought her something. Helen learned, in this situation as in many others throughout her young life, that fighting to win by any means usually got the conflict resolved the way she wanted. It temporarily dispelled her fear, and reassured her of her position in the family.

In the same shoe-buying incident, Susan and Penny were left with both a feeling of relief that the conflict was over, and a resentment that they had been dumped on unfairly, manipulated to "even the score." They had fought knowing they would lose.

An alternative scenario

The whole thing might have been handled differently. It might have gone something like this (though it would probably have taken longer):

Mother: (identifying Helen's feeling) You're really angry because Penny got something you didn't? (A simple sentence like this can express a belief that we are accepted and loved by God even when we have negative feelings.)

Helen: (furious) Yeah!

Mother: You think I love her more than I love you?

Helen: (Stubborn silence)

Mother: I bought her two pairs of shoes and none for you.

Helen: It's not fair! (sobbing)

Mother: Okay, you feel it's not fair. You have a right to your feelings. You have every right to be angry or upset. But you don't have a right to take those feelings out on us.

Helen: (sniff)

Mother: You are responsible for your own feelings. And we will not take your abuse. We do want to talk to you about your feelings. But we don't know if you'll listen, when you think I'm mean and you hate your sister. And I feel hurt because you think I'm mean for buying Penny shoes.

Susan would have to show Helen that she's not taking sides. With Penny, in the presence of her older sister Helen, the situation might have been handled like this:

Mother: You aren't very happy right now.

Penny: Helen told me she hated me! How would she like to be the one who has to go to a million stores before she finds a decent pair of shoes that fit?

Mother: You find shopping for shoes pretty upsetting?

Penny: Yes! And Helen's temper too!
Mother: Helen, do you understand how Penny feels
about this?

Assert your position, allow freedom of response

But suppose Helen refuses to listen. Suppose she continues
her blaming and insults. After all, she's playing to win, by
any means. In that situation, Susan and nine-year-old Penny
may have to leave the room. But not yelling or sulking. That
would be playing Helen's game, Helen's way. Susan and
Penny may need to say, clearly but firmly, "We can't continue this discussion if you won't listen and respect our
feelings."

There's a risk here. Mother accepted Helen's feelings
earlier; now she's isolating her. Helen may feel rejected as
well as threatened. But she may also learn that people can't
keep attending to her feelings if she won't attend to theirs.

Susan and Penny needn't tell 11-year-old Helen what to do
or how to respond. They just have to let her know how her
behavior affects them. Then they leave it up to her to take
responsibility for her response.

Helen, for her part, might simply withdraw. She may never
mention that discussion again. But the next time a conflict
comes up, she may react differently, indicating that she did
take their words and feelings to heart.

If Helen has had a lot of "wins" from her style of dealing
with conflict, she may not change her behavior easily. Susan
and Penny may have to repeat this routine, over and over,
until Helen learns that blaming, insulting and demanding will
no longer get a "win" for her.

There's always the possibility that Helen may never
change. That too is a risk. There are limits to how long
anyone can keep on trying to respond lovingly. But one of the
lessons we can learn from the Bible is that one party doesn't
quit, just because the other has.

Almost the whole of the Old Testament has a single great

theme—God's faithfulness, even when the people of Israel proved unfaithful. We may not be able to live up to God's standard, but we need to try. Mother and sister need to persist in expressing their conflicting needs and feelings, for the sake of love and justice, and for the sake of their own mental health so they don't explode into fiercer conflict from repressed resentment. And Helen needs to be offered feedback on her behavior, feedback which offers her an opportunity to reflect and change—just as the prophets gave God's feedback to the Hebrew people.

But note that in this situation, when Mother and Penny need to support each other as they continue to confront Helen, they do so for Helen's benefit, not to form an alliance against her. It's like friends getting together to convince someone to get help for a drinking problem. Or team members gathering to restrain an athlete itching for a fight. It's harder for angry people to deny their destructive behavior, to think they're right and someone else is wrong, when more than one other person sees it differently.

And to avoid making Helen feel excluded as a member of the family, Mother and Helen, or Penny and Helen, could team up for enjoyable activities like going to a movie.

Establish ways of resolving conflict

If Helen does respond through conversation and admits her feelings and fears, Susan and Penny could talk with her to find out how to avoid situations which make her feel so threatened. Things might go like this:

Helen: I guess I get carried away when Penny gets things and I don't. It makes me think she's your favorite.

Mother: What could Penny and I do and say another time so you won't get so upset? Maybe if we had asked something about you knowing how hard it is for Penny to find nice shoes that fit her? And that we were lucky to find some?

Helen: That sounds better.
Mother: And what could you say another time, Helen, when you're upset?
Helen: Maybe…uh… It's hard not to feel jealous when Penny gets things and I don't—even when I know she needs them.
Mother: That would help a lot.

Start young

Knowing Helen and Susan as well as I do, I realize that it would take a great deal of strength for Susan to stand up to her daughter this way. Helen has a strong personality. She has established a pattern of defensive behavior that has worked for her for many years. She won't change that behavior easily. In fact, it may get worse before it gets better. Helen may well try a double or triple dose of the behavior that worked for her in the past before she decides to try a new way.

We can help to prevent defensive behavior patterns like Helen's from developing if we start the process of identifying and dealing with conflict when our children are very young. A crying baby may not understand when his father (after checking carefully that he hasn't stuck a diaper pin into his infant!) says, "You're crying because you know I'm going out and you want me to stay. I have to go out to buy us some food. Remember I love you and I will come back." But this kind of "baby-talk" builds a foundation for the child's future ability to identify feelings and needs in conflict situations. In time, that baby will also learn, from parental example and experience, the other skills required in dealing with conflict.

Applying learnings about conflict

Although it may take strength for us and for our children to deal with conflict in our families, the kind of words I've suggested here are gentle and accepting compared to the words of the prophets and of Jesus when they confronted people who chose not to live God's way and to hold on to position and power. Our children will meet "whited sepulchres" and "evildoers" too—on playgrounds, in classrooms, at part-time jobs. They will be able to apply the conflict resolving principles and skills they learned at home. But those principles and skills won't always work in the same way.

Families or close friends often have a commitment to stay together and to work through differences to the satisfaction of all. Other contexts may lack that commitment. Playground bullies, teachers, supervisors in summer jobs, may all use their strength and power and status to fulfill their own needs at the expense of others. Such people may not care if they stay in relationship with our children or treat their needs justly.

This is when our children need help to be "wise as serpents and gentle as doves." Like Jesus, they may need to respond differently in different situations.

With the bully in the playground, they may have to figure out the feelings, fears and needs of the bully rather than seeing him as "all bad." Maybe he needs attention and can't get it by doing well in the classroom. His defense is to overcome physically those whom he fears consider themselves better than him academically. Some positive attention to the bully might diminish his need for aggressiveness.

With an unfair teacher or boss, our children may need to get together with fellow students or employees. Then, as a group, they may have to express their needs and feelings over and over again to appropriate authorities who could influence the situation.

And, of course, sometimes it *is* better to avoid the conflict. Changing classes or jobs makes its own statement.

Constant reflection and practice in conflict situations, with our help, will enable children to know intuitively what to do. They will also learn that sometimes, no matter how well they analyze and act, the conflict may never be resolved. We learned that in our family when my husband and I separated.

No techniques could create the compatibility necessary to make our marriage work. Painful as it was to face our differences, we were able to accept that the differences were so great that the best way to deal with our conflicts was to avoid them and not live together. Because we accepted our differences—rather than rejecting them and putting others down—we've been able to relate amicably. And Nancy and Bryan can say with assurance that they would not want us living together in conflict again, for our own sakes and theirs.

Faced with conflict, our children need to know that they must do what is loving and just without any guarantee about how the other person will respond. Families may break up, friendships may fall apart; teams may split up. We need to support our children when they take a stand and assure them that God is with them when they do the loving thing—hard as it is to love our enemies.

Out into the world

As children mature, they will become more conscious of systems in the world that conflict with the ideals that you have taught them. They will have to use their skills to deal with conflicts around issues such as human rights for all races, dignity for the sick and dying, empowering the poor, nuclear disarmament.

It won't be easy. But they will be following the example of their parents and of Jesus—who was killed by those who fought to "win" and to hold onto power. Fortunately, we know the end of that story, and our children must know it too. Love and justice never die. God is always with those who love. They will never be ultimately defeated. New life always comes from loving action—for those who love and for the world.

CHAPTER FIVE

Crises, support, and renewal

by Donna Sinclair

Every family has crises. Ours run past my inner vision like a silent film, in no particular order, chronological or of importance. There was the time David, at about four or five, nearly drowned. One minute he was there, the next he had disappeared into some deep, underwater hole while we were at the beach. Jim raced to the spot, reached under and pulled him out, while I stood paralyzed, clutching his younger brother at the edge of the water.

"You came as fast as you could, Dad," he said, once he had sputtered his way back to coherence.

And there was the infinitely darker time when Andy, at 14, went off to train at a university swim camp 300 miles away. He and his friend were staying at a university residence when they were attacked, robbed and in danger of being killed. We survived that crisis too, thanks to friends who lived in that

*city, who enveloped Andy and his friend with all the care in
the world.*

*There was the move from Cowansville to North Bay, the
guinea pigs on the floor beside me, the back of the station
wagon piled high with house plants, the dog between the two
boys on the back seat, all of us crying for the familiar, comforting things we were leaving behind.*

*There was the time David fell off the ski hill and broke his
arm so badly he had to have a steel plate inserted.*

There was Grandpa dying…

There are many different kinds of crises. All of them are
stressful and painful and difficult to get through. Some are
natural, "predictable" crises: we knew that Grandpa would die
one day, we know that moving is part of many modern
families' lives. We prepare ourselves for these predictable
crises unconsciously. Grandpa's death is accompanied by the
funeral ritual; moving is accompanied by the farewell rituals
of goodbye parties, and eased by the welcoming gestures by
neighbors in a new place.

Other crises are more random. A child is born handicapped, parents divorce, someone is raped, cancer strikes the
youngest member of the family. A viciousness that lurks
somewhere in a far corner of the universe explodes into our
lives.

But they are all crises—times of bitterness, confusion, fear,
grief. And they all have one thing in common. Our true view
of God, our understanding of the way God is, surfaces and
becomes terribly important at this point. If we regard God as
essentially loving, our children will be raised lovingly, and
will feel assured of God's nurturing even during times of
great pain. If we regard God as punishing and vengeful, we
will rule our children with an iron hand, and in times of crisis,
we will wonder what we have done to deserve the iron hand
of God raised against us. If we regard God as all-powerful,
we and our children will have a difficult time understanding

why God would do this to the innocent.

So how do we get a child, and a family, through a crisis? And how do we see God in that process?

Freeing a child from guilt

The first thing is to look at some crises and try to figure out what the child needs in order to survive. One component surfaced for me as I sat in my nine-year-old daughter's room. Tracy wanted me to sit with her while she got dressed, because Max had died in the night. Max was her special goldfish, a black one with googly eyes. Max's features made him stand out in her aquarium.

The other three fish were all gold with long graceful tails and eyes set in their heads in the way we are used to. We were all fond of Max. Maybe all of us have moments of identifying with the odd person (fish) out.

Anyway, Tracy wasn't doing much dressing for school. She and I sat on the edge of her bed, gazing at the aquarium with its three remaining occupants. Tracy was snuffling. Her brother came in, alerted by her tears. In the bathroom, Dad performed funeral rites on the fish (the toilet flushed in the small bathroom).

> **Andy:** What's happened? One of the goldfish died?
> **Tracy:** Max (sniff) died.
> **Andy:** Isn't that amazing! That goldfish lived over two years in this house. That must be longer than any goldfish *ever* lived. He must have set some kind of record!
> **Tracy:** (silence, but she has stopped crying.)
> **Andy:** You really know how to take care of goldfish, Tracy.

Tracy got up, put on her clothes, cheerfully ate her breakfast, and went to school.

Her 16-year-old brother had provided what she had needed to survive the crisis, while her mother (who writes about children's issues) and her father (a minister) had been struck dumb. Tracy needed to be relieved of her sense of guilt because the small creature in her care had died. Maybe Max had died because she had fed him too much or too little. Maybe—oh horrible thought—she hadn't loved him enough.

Guilt is a component in many grief situations, not just this one. It's compounded by the fact that children feel they are the centre of the universe. And, of course, they are. Usually, it takes either maturity or the birth of your own child to force you to move over from that centre. So a child might think something like, *"If I am the centre of the universe, surely it was up to me to stop this. Perhaps I have offended God who is in charge, and that is why this happened."*

We see the same dynamic in children who feel guilty when their parents divorce: "Maybe if I hadn't fought with Cindy, they would have been happier together, and this wouldn't have happened." Or when someone they love dies.

Children need to know clearly that they are not to blame. Andy supplied it in our case. Tracy had *not* caused Max's death. God was *not* punishing her by taking Max away.

Recognizing a child's crisis

I had been doing one thing right, though. I had at least been sitting quietly with Tracy. I had, at some level, known what parents sometimes don't recognize—that while the death of a goldfish may not be a crisis for an adult, it *is* a crisis for a child.

I can't take a lot of credit for that insight. I had spent some time in the previous year talking with a friend of mine, Rev. Karen Mitchell, about her experiences offering pastoral care to the children in her congregation. "What may seem like a minor event to us," she had explained, "isn't always so minor to the child. But since ministers and parents are usually adults, sometimes children don't receive pastoral care at times when they really need it." Especially since they aren't always able to name their problem very well. Tracy had not, for instance, said to me, "Mom, I really feel guilty. Maybe Max died because I wasn't a good goldfish-keeper."

When a group of children wrote to Kidpower (*The United Church Observer*'s children's page) about their crises—"the things that would be really hard for you, when you would want an adult or minister to help you"—I asked Karen to write replies to them. Some of their crises seemed unimportant; but she recognized how crucial they were.

"Once I left my bike behind my Mom's car," wrote Cam. "The tire got bent. It is hard for me, because I just got it a couple of days ago."

"Dear Cam," Karen answered. "It really hurts when you have a brand new thing and it gets broken. I bet you were really excited when you got the new bike, and really sad when it got bent. "

She had heard Cam's concern clearly. He was rightly concerned about the damage to his most cherished possession. (For adults to understand, substitute "new car" for "new bike" and "door bashed in" for "tire bent.") Behind that, though, she heard even deeper questions, ones Cam may not have been aware of himself. Like Tracy, wondering if she had been a good goldfish-keeper, and unable to put that question into words, Cam may have wondered, "How mad *is* Mom at me? Is this going to destroy our relationship? Am I a hopelessly careless human being?"

Karen responded compassionately to those deeper questions, too. "Accidents happen so easy and so fast. Your Mom probably felt really bad too. She may have been angry and upset because the bike was new, but she also may have been afraid that you were there too. It's a good thing you weren't hurt." (If Mom is mad, it's because she cares about you. Therefore your relationship with her is safe.)

"Sometimes," Karen went on, "we need to learn from the bad stuff that happens to us. The bike was new. It cost a lot of money, and it hurt everyone to see it bent. I hope you were able to get the bike fixed. I can tell you'll never forget it."

(You aren't hopelessly careless and stupid. You can learn from this incident. Your feelings of sadness are justified. And now you are an infinitely wiser person—you won't forget this.)

This is a terribly important skill for any parent to have— the ability to recognize the child's legitimate pain—not brush it off, but respond to it in a deep sense. The least helpful response here would have been name-calling: "What a stupid, careless child you are!" That would have simply reinforced the unspoken fear in Cam's mind.

Almost as unhelpful would have been to ignore his pain: "It's only a bent tire! What are you crying about? You'll soon grow out of that bike, anyway!"

Most helpful was to face the consequences of his action, and accept his feelings: "The bike was new... it got bent... it cost money... you are sad." Then you can offer hope: "I hope you were able to get it fixed. I can tell you won't forget this."

This process requires listening at several levels, trying to make sure you have gotten to the very bottom of the crisis, to the most deeply hidden fear. It's not easy, but you'll find it is as helpful and comforting to your adult friends as to your children. You can practise it on adults too.

Providing respect and support

Equally important in a crisis is respect, support, awareness of the dignity of those who have been struck by crisis. I remember—oh, so clearly—the time when Andy and his friend were beaten, robbed and left terrified in a university residence where we had thought they would be safe. That was a crisis for adults too.

The two boys had persuaded us that a summer swim camp at a university would be good for their aquatic careers. So off they went, only to find themselves the victims of one of those random acts of violence that sometimes slash into the lives of the innocent. It made me feel, later, as if evil is like some kind of irrational comet that races out of control through the universe, spewing little chunks of madness all over the place.

One of those little chunks hit the boys in the form of a tough, street-wise wanderer, souped up on narcotics and armed with a sharpened screwdriver. He wandered into their room, demanded money, tied them up, and threatened to kill them.

The boys fought and yelled for a nightmare twenty minutes—choked, half-strangled, punched, one of them blinded by a pillowcase over his head. The one man who heard them from the room next door didn't know what was going on, and did nothing.

Andy wrote out the experience later:

"He ripped the straps off a few of the bags and he began to tie us up. He grabbed me by the hair and hit me really hard on the side of the head. 'I know you have money. Where is it? Don't fuck with me!'

"I told him over and over that was all I had, and he still wouldn't believe me, so I started to cry... He went into the bathroom. 'Do you have any razors...' We yelled. But the man grabbed both of us, each neck surrounded by one of his arms, and started to strangle us; he started to squeeze really hard and I saw spots in front of my eyes. I couldn't breathe. I pulled on his arm. My hands had not been bound well. I pulled his hair and struggled."

Finally, a woman resident passing down the hall heard their frantic pleas for help and alerted the reception desk. When a group of women gathered outside the door, the man coolly walked out of the room and out of the residence. He was later arrested, still carrying the boys' wallets.

This crisis was handled well.

First, the seven police on the case all treated the boys with dignity and respect. No guilt. They didn't ask: "Why didn't you lock your room immediately when you entered?" They didn't imply any guilt: "Did you encourage him in any way?"

Instead, they helped the boys feel like the survivors they were, praised them for the way they had helped each other and for the way they finally managed, despite the intruder's threats, to attract attention and scare him away.

Second, they were immediately taken in hand by friends of ours in the city who surrounded them with affection, care and talking time. Communities of friends are crucial in surviving crises. Our friends had the wisdom to provide writing materials and encourage them to get the whole story down, so that by the time we arrived early the next morning, the story was there in black and white. The boys weren't tempted to edit it to spare our feelings; it was there, and we could read it, and know the whole story, and enter into its horror with them. No one pretended it hadn't happened. Everyone was simply with them.

Our friends provided food, especially pasta, which swimmers eat in large quantities. No one said "You'll be stronger for this," or "Your being spared must be part of some plan God has for you." They would have greeted either assertion with the skepticism it deserved. The nurturing God we believe in does not provide crises and pain. That kind of thing comes without God's affirmation.

The final and most important part of that intuitive respect and support the boys received was to be made part of the decision-making process. Nobody—not the police, not ourselves, not the doctors who examined them, and not our friends—suggested that the adults knew best. Everyone waited for the boys to decide what they wanted to do.

What they wanted to do was swim. So our friends provided a spare bedroom for the duration of the week, lots more pasta and other delicious things, and set them free in the city (which they could be pardoned for regarding as a jungle) again, to go to swim camp.

It was a healing process—possibly because of the wisdom of the adults involved, and of the boys themselves.

Rituals, ceremonies, and chicken soup

In addition to random, inexplicable crises, there's a whole range of crises for which we are—in a way—prepared. Not that these are any easier to deal with. But the rituals which surround them offer a sense of order that counteracts the randomness.

When Grandpa died, for example, there was a funeral. For the children, a funeral was a new experience. They hadn't been to one before. Still, things fell into a pattern. Everyone knew—and the children learned quickly—what was appropriate behavior.

There were tears. Even in the most WASP of families, tears and hugs are appropriate. Children in grief need to take part in that.

There were neighbors, bringing food, offering places to sleep for the relatives. The loving acts of the community are part of the ritual of the death of a beloved member of the community.

There were conversations, reflections on the life of someone crucial to the family, our father, husband, grandfather, uncle, brother. Memories were shaped, strengthened, crystallized. Reflection—alone and together—is part of the ritual of death. Children can be part of that too.

There was the waiting at the coffin. Depending on the custom of the family, many families have visiting hours at the funeral home, where the memories are shared again, and people who had even a peripheral place in Grandpa's life can come and share a few words about what he meant to them. Overhearing this, the children share part of his life they may not have known, one which strengthens their own roots.

Finally, there was the church, the words of the service, the sense that death had happened before and would happen again. This death was placed in the context of our faith. We reaffirmed that there is a God, that this is part of the order of things. And we heard that there would be a resurrection— Grandpa's resurrection and our own. We would feel whole again some day. The service, with its reminder of God's covenant, was part of the accepted order of things.

So chaos, randomness and the presence of evil were held at bay by prayers, comfort, community, memories, and the transcendent presence of God. Ritual is healing, for children as well as adults.

Also important, in these rituals of crisis, is what is said and not said. If you are fortunate, when your own family's crisis of death comes along, no one will say to your children, "Well, Grandpa is needed in heaven," or, "God loved Grandpa so much he wanted Grandpa with him in heaven." Both statements—as well as presenting God as both selfish and male—raise a terrible question for the child: "Didn't *I* need Grandpa enough, didn't *I* love him enough?"

And if you are fortunate, no one will say, "It's all part of God's plan." As one of friend of mine—having been through a crisis of her own—declared, "I can't somehow see God sitting somewhere, brooding away over some devious plan to make me suffer. God *doesn't* decide to give out tragedies."

Again it is a question of our view of God. And this might be a good place to write a statement, again. What is God like? How does the God I believe in act? This is our statement. Perhaps it will lead you to write your own.

- *The God we believe in doesn't plan someone's death.* God doesn't "take them home," or—most especially—give them cancer so they can be "relieved of their suffering by death."
- *The God we believe in simply mourns with us* when we are separated from our loved ones.
- *The God we believe in doesn't punish people.* People may drink themselves to death or smoke or not take care of themselves, and those bring certain, almost inevitable, consequences. But God doesn't arrange for them to die. Most particularly, people who lead a reprehensible life, or don't love their parents enough, or don't work hard enough, do not

get punished for that by a crisis of some kind. God doesn't work that way.

If you accept all that, some other principles may follow:

• *The God we believe in may not be all-powerful.* This is frightening, but we need to look at the possibility. Surely an all-powerful *loving* God would not have allowed the Holocaust, would not let parents lose the child they love, would not countenance a young mother dying from leukemia.

It follows then—if God is not utterly autonomous—that God somehow requires *us* to care for the world and to love one another. God cannot or will not do it all. We are co-creators.

Paradoxically, however, *God is far, far more powerful than we can imagine.* God has infinitely more than human power, and we can call on that power in times of crisis.

• At the same time, *God is with us.* God feels our pain, and is not dislodged by it. God weeps for our suffering, but is not incapacitated by it. God loves us deeply, profoundly, passionately.

• *God can handle our anger.* We don't have to pretend. Of course, if God did "take away" Grandpa, that *would* be good cause for anger. If we've been lucky enough to avoid well-meaning people who proffer that advice, we may be spared much needless rage. But sometimes love does involve anger. And God's love is strong enough to take it.

For a fuller treatment of all this, read the excellent and widely available book by Harold Kushner: *When Bad Things Happen to Good People* (Schocken).

Crises with no rituals—like divorce

If ritual eases some kinds of crises, it follows that crises for which there is no ritual will be more difficult for your children. That's one reason why separation and divorce are so awkward to deal with. One child, for instance, familiar with the ways of funerals, found himself in a home where the father had simply left. He turned to his mother and inquired, "Where are the neighbors, bringing in the soup?"

Emotionally drained parents don't always have the inner resources to provide rituals which can take the place of the procession of food-bearers.

So what can we do? I believe that some of the events of divorce (helping one parent move, for instance) can take on aspects of ritual, expressing a finality and sense of concreteness that the child needs, painful though the activity may be.

And some farsighted churches (you might ask your minister about this, if you are facing this kind of crisis in your family) have developed liturgies for use in a service of worship which might help the community recognize the new situation. The congregation can then respond to the new situation, as well as do the necessary theological reflection following a crisis.

"Where is God in all this?" is the legitimate question of the divorcing family. God is where God is in any crisis: broken, suffering with them, and still assuring them of love. Look at Mark's description of Jesus' experience with the disciples on the water:

> So they left the crowd; the disciples got into the boat in which Jesus was already sitting, and they took him with them. Other boats were there too. Suddenly a strong wind blew up, and the waves began to spill over into the boat, so that it was about to fill with water. Jesus was in the back of the boat, sleeping with his head on a pillow. The disciples woke him up and said, "Teacher, don't you care that we are about to die?"
>
> Jesus stood up and commanded the wind, "Be quiet!" and he said to the waves, "Be still!" The wind

died down, and there was a great calm. Then Jesus
said to his disciples, "Why are you frightened? Do you
still have no faith?"

(Mark 4:36–40, *Good News Bible*)

There's a strong sense of God's continuing presence in that
passage. Or you might find reassurance in the way Jesus wept
at Lazarus' death, as a way of understanding how God
mourns with us, and is related to us.

And with all children, it's all right to share your feelings.
Yes, we wonder where God is. Yes, we are sad. We may even
be angry at God. But we trust that God is strong enough to
accept our anger, and that God will be with us.

With older children, you might remind yourselves of the
story of the Resurrection. The night is dark, but we are told
over and over that there is light even there. Healing and
wholeness and new life do come after the old life is gone.
These deaths are painful, but they are not permanent.

You may have to find for yourself and your children a
spiritual counselor, one who can help you hold on to that idea
of God's continuing presence in the darkest times. Don't try
to survive this time alone. The disciples couldn't survive their
dark times alone; why should you?

In any case, you can see that there is a firm relationship
between our understanding of God and our understanding of
child-rearing. God does not stand apart from us, judging and
pointing out failures in relationship. God is with us, encouraging and accepting, not trying to shield us from a necessary
ending, but standing by.

I can amplify that belief a bit more by describing yet
another family crisis.

Sometimes we bring it on ourselves

Once when we were away, our adolescents had a party.
And what a party it was! Incredibly noisy, crowded, boozy
and completely unauthorized. The neighbors eventually called

the police, the boys cleaned up, and we came home, all unknowing, to a spotless house.

We didn't remain in innocence forever, though. (Innocent as doves and as sly as serpents are good characteristics for the parents of adolescents. Be alert when you come home and the house is *too* clean.) I found a beer bottle cap under the piano. My husband found another under the sofa. We dug another out of the flower bed, and found three or four more on top of a cupboard. A few small ornaments were out of place, and some had disappeared. (I found them later in a drawer.) I finally realized that everything valuable that could be broken had been packed up and put away for the party. Given the type of party it had been, that was a wise move.

We confronted the boys. "Why did you do that?" we wanted to know. "How could you do that to us behind our backs? We've always been straight with you. Why weren't you straight with us?"

It was a shattering time. Only a party, yes. But our trust, our faith in their honesty, our understanding of their good sense, seemed to have gone out the window. Could we ever trust each other again? In every other family crisis we had had each other. In this one we were separated from each other, confused, angry and hurt.

How were we as parents to handle it? How are parents to handle *any* crisis—drugs, addiction, theft, whatever—where our values are wounded and we feel terribly damaged, betrayed?

Again, our view of God shaped the way we handled it as we did.

- *We did not punish them*. At least not directly. "Are you going to ground us?" one of them asked—the standard punishment for most of his friends. But if you don't believe in a punishing God, you won't especially believe in punishment. "No," we said. "That wouldn't do any good. But we can't leave you alone again, either." So...

• *They had to face the consequences of their action themselves.* That meant that they had to accompany us to whatever out of town event we were going to for the next year or so, or make other arrangements. They couldn't be trusted alone with the house. So they had to attend some functions they would rather have avoided.

For children whose acting-out is more severe— like frequently coming home drunk at all hours, refusing to have anything to do with family tasks or meals, affecting other children—the consequences might mean simply being told the house could no longer be theirs until they were in a better space.

Note the difference between punishment and consequences. Although it may seem subtle, it's there. Being removed from the house is not done to "teach them a lesson." It's the necessary conse- quence of behavior that affects the rest of the family adversely.

Part of the consequences following the party, in our case, were that

• *They had to cope with our anger and disappoint- ment.* We are a close family. Having Mom hurt and depressed is not pleasant. I made no attempt to hide the fact I was in pain over this. This was not com- fortable for them.

• However, I think it was clear that *we had not stopped loving them*, nor that we thought they were bad kids. We thoroughly disapproved of their *actions*. But we still loved *them*.

That's the way God is with us. God does not punish us. Whatever your conscience may say when you have a crisis, God is *not* punishing you for failing to attend church, or for not visiting Aunt Allie, or for swearing. God doesn't work like that. Your actions may bring consequences in them- selves, of course. If you step off the top of a tall building,

God doesn't punish you by making you go splat on the side-
walk; you simply experience the consequences of your own
actions. Not going to church may deprive us of community
and one way of finding meaning in life. Not visiting Aunt
Allie may deprive us of a pleasant relationship. Swearing may
offend someone's ears, and even cause them to avoid you.
God may be hurt by all those things. But God doesn't punish
us for them. And God always continues to love us, despite our
actions.

So where does this leave us? I need to say one thing—or to
repeat it, because I have said it before. In every crisis, however dark, there is the hope of eventual re-birth and renewal.
Crises are very dark times, but they are also turning points,
the start of new life.

Take the story of Jairus' daughter. It has all the elements of
crisis we have mentioned:

> Jesus went back across to the other side of the lake....
> Jairus, an official of the local synagogue, arrived and
> when he saw Jesus, he threw himself down at his feet
> and begged him earnestly, "My little daughter is very
> sick. Please come and place your hands on her, so that
> she will get well and live!"
>
> Then Jesus started off with him....
>
> Some messengers came from Jairus' house and
> told him, "Your daughter has died. Why bother the
> Teacher any longer?"
>
> Jesus paid no attention to what they said, but told
> him, "Don't be afraid, only believe." Then he did not
> let anyone else go on with him except Peter and James
> and his brother John. They arrived at Jairus' house,
> where Jesus saw the confusion and heard all the loud
> crying and wailing. He went in and said to them, "Why
> all this confusion? Why are you crying? The
> child is not dead—she is only sleeping! "
>
> They started making fun of him, so he put them all
> out, took the child's father and mother and his three

disciples, and went into the room where the child was lying. He took her by the hand and said to her...
"Little girl, I tell you to get up."
    She got up at once and started walking around.
(She was twelve years old.) When this happened, they were completely amazed. But Jesus gave them strict orders not to tell anyone, and he said, "Give her something to eat."
                (Mark 5:21–24, 35–43, *Good News Bible*)

This biblical passage is a wonderful model for the handling of a crisis.

- The father understood the need for *support*, and was not embarrassed to ask for it—even from a wandering holy man whom some would regard with suspicion.
- There was *no sense of guilt or punishment*—Jesus could have scolded the father, and said, "I'm busy now. Can't you see I'm with all these people? Why didn't you come sooner?" or, "Why didn't you look after her better?" Instead he simply set his other concerns aside and came, bringing hope.
- The parents were surrounded by a *network* of concerned friends.
- And the child in the crisis was treated with *dignity and respect*. Jesus addressed her directly. Furthermore, Jesus had a knack for figuring out what the child might *feel but not say*. "Give her something to eat," he said, when she stood up. That's careful listening.

This passage doesn't show us how to keep a child from dying; in some family crises, the child *is* dying, or blind or deaf or crippled, and there is no cure. There comes that metaphorical comet again, snaking through the universe scattering pain and sorrow randomly. But this passage shows that after a crisis—no matter what the outcome—the possibility of resurrection, some form of new life, some new beginnings in God exists.

As writer Jean Little explains in her autobiography *Little by Little* (Viking Kestrel) it's not necessary to have miraculous cures for people to find new life. She wondered, while she was teaching permanently handicapped children, "Why couldn't there be a happy ending without a miracle cure? Why wasn't there a story with a child in it who resembled the kids I taught?"

Her particular re-birth came in writing those stories, wonderful, touching, profoundly true stories which made her—despite her own extreme visual handicap—beloved by children all over North America and Europe.

There is resurrection. Children and adults who are deadened by the loss of a grandparent, or by the different shape of their family after a divorce, or by the moving away of a best friend, or who are abused or frightened, can still—with support and respect and love—come alive again. Like Jairus' daughter, we can become people who can walk on our own. "Don't be afraid," explains Jesus, "only have faith." Without denying our pain and fear, those words can help to get us through a crisis.

CHAPTER SIX

Being different, being accepted, and being faithful

by Yvonne Stewart

When my 22-year-old son, Bryan, and I moved from our apartment into a house, we discovered, to his horror, that his room was the only place where my huge bookcase would fit. The bookcase itself was not the problem. My rather extensive collection of religious books stored on it was. Bryan worried that visitors looking around his room would think the books were his, and would assume he was "weird" or "different."

Being religious and being part of a community of faith can often set us apart as "different" in our secular western society today—especially if we try to live out the principles of our faith. So Christian parents have the challenge of communicating and living their faith in ways that help their children find enough meaning and love in their lives to compensate for being "different" in society.

Being part of a Christian family makes them—and us—different.

But not only do we need to provide our children with a sense of self-esteem in society, we need to do so in a church that often considers children "different." They are viewed as lesser members who don't yet know enough or contribute enough to have earned the status of full members of the congregation. In many churches, children meet in the basement while adults worship upstairs. Children are rarely consulted when decisions are made about their programs, let alone about the work of the church as a whole. They are often forgotten when family crises such as divorce or death occur. Parents get pastoral visits and counseling, not children.

Some churches are beginning to include children in their life and work. We need to celebrate this and work to further this acceptance. Our children will not bother paying the cost of being "different" in society, if their church excludes them and refuses the gifts and talents they offer to the community of faith.

Will our children choose to be different?

Even if we do all we can at home and in the congregation, our children may still choose not to journey in faith with us and with the church. Remember Bryan and the bookcase? He was afraid people would think him "different"—not because he was religious, but because he *wasn't*. They might get the wrong impression.

I did my best to ensure that he felt a part of the community of faith (and he agrees that I did—to the point of threatening to take him to church in his pyjamas if he wasn't ready on time). And I tried to make sure he knew something of the beliefs, mission, stories and rituals of this community of faith. But he does not want to be a part of it at this time of his life. He also hates to admit how much he loved church when he was little.

So, no matter how hard or how well we try, there are no

guarantees that our children will accept the "differentness" of a committed intentional Christian lifestyle.

Our children seek their own identity

In fact, if our children know how important our faith is to us, it may be on this very point that they choose to separate from us and find their own identity as young adults. Bryan, for example, needed to find an identity apart from me—a strong mother who has been deeply involved in religious matters all his life. So he sought to discover himself and life's meaning, first by rejecting religion and the church, then by exploring other venues. He tried world travel on his own, lived by the values of his friends rather than his mother, and tested philosophies of life that differed from the ones he grew up with.

Bryan also searched for meaning outside of religion because he was influenced by the self-reliant, strong male image that society still pushes at men today. On TV, fiction and documentaries, commercials and advertisements, often portray men who seem able to solve all of life's problems with money, brains, technology, physical strength, ambition, power. For this kind of male to need God—a power beyond himself—seems less than macho. So if a young boy wants to be a real man he doesn't lean on anyone, not even God.

But even though Bryan is anything but explicit about Christian values, he lives by those values. He cares about underdogs and defends their rights for justice. He'll argue vehemently with those who want to keep people of different races out of our country, and with those who don't want to contribute money or taxes for the elderly, the sick, the disabled, the poor. The list goes on.

My daughter also went through a time in her early teens when she deeply questioned the faith. Nancy felt she couldn't believe in what she couldn't see and prove—a feeling common to many adolescents. Although I still can't say she's deeply committed to the church in her mid-20s, she's happy

to consider herself a member of a congregation and to participate in some of its activities. She has even taken courses in
religion at university! Religion never threatened her identity
as a woman as it did my male child. Connectedness with
another, for good or for ill, has been part of being female.

The tension between culture and religion

Our culture has a fairly low assessment of religious people
(unless you're Mother Teresa). Parents raising children in a
Christian lifestyle have to contend with that assessment. They
also have to contend with society's definitions of what it
means to be male and female. And with much more. The
consumer approach to Christian high holidays, for instance,
teaches our children what they can *get* from Santa or the
Easter Bunny on these special days, but nothing about the
actual story behind the celebration, or about the lifestyle we
are really called to live because of Christmas and Easter.

As well, modern society offers many exciting alternatives
to Sabbath rest and going to church on Sunday. Almost anything you can name sounds more appealing to young people
than prayer and study of scripture. Giving away one-tenth of
one's free time, talent, and money makes little sense to young
people who can see so many other things to do and to buy.
Nor does speaking out with oppressed people such as the
homeless at a Saturday afternoon political meeting appeal to
them—especially if their summer jobs as government
employees might be on the line, or they're missing a chance
to windsurf.

We and our children have many temptations before us as
we struggle to decide whether and how to live out Christian
values.

What has the faith got going for it?

Is there anything going for us and for our faith that might
have an impact on our children? Yes. Many people today—
young and old—recognize that the future of creation is in

jeopardy. We humans are polluting and destroying the natural environment. We have also built up an arsenal of weapons that could annihilate the world thousands of times over. People are in violent combat with one another in many regions. The problems seem overwhelming and unresolvable.

People are realizing that we need a creative force beyond our human limits to give us the hope and strength and vision to save creation, to choose life over death. Some of us call that force God. We turn to the power of this loving God for help in healing our world.

Parents can offer their children an exciting opportunity—to discover God at work in the world, and to join with God in the task of healing creation. Note that we can only *offer*. God invites us to "choose this day whom we will serve" (Joshua 24:15). We, including our children, have the freedom to decide and to take the consequences of our decisions.

Our children will serve God in their own way...

If our children do decide to serve God, they may not do so in ways that we parents would. They may not do it through a church, especially if a congregation seems more concerned about its own maintenance and survival rather than caring for God's world.

Our children may get involved in the peace movement or environmental issues *instead,* even though we might like them to do this *as well as* coming to church.

...but they will be affected

If you do belong to a community of faith that does take action on behalf of God's people and world, you and your children (willing or not) may sometimes have to pay a cost. Congregational leaders in U.S. churches that provided sanctuary to Central American refugees have been spied upon, arrested, and tried for their actions. The children of these people are inevitably involved. They too suffer the consequences of their parents' and the faith community's actions.

They may be ostracized by people who disagree with the sanctuary movement. They may suffer the results of reduced family income because of costly legal fees. They may even lose a parent for the duration of a prison term. Many of us remember the price paid by Christians in the confessing church in Germany who opposed Hitler's policies of genocide.

Even when children disagree with their parents' faith stance, they will get "flak." A good friend is a prominent peace activist. Her son chose a career in the military. When he applied for post-graduate studies in missiles and armaments, his acceptance was delayed because of his mother's peace involvement.

Today, Christian communities who gather for worship and Bible study in Central and South American countries, such as Guatemala, risk persecution and death because their Christian principles lead them to criticize the actions of their governments. Christian groups opposed to apartheid in South Africa face similar prospects. Yet in all these instances, the faith still has something going for it. It offers hope to the oppressed. These Christians feel it is worth taking risks for the sake of God's people.

If children have to pay the costs of a community of faith's risk-taking just as much as adult members, then they need to be as fully informed and involved as anyone else. They are also part of the body of Christ. They need to receive the joy, strength, and courage that is present when two or three gather in Christ's name.

Many Christian denominations symbolize children's inclusion in the body of Christ by practicing infant baptism. Baptism is the sole rite of initiation into the church. When our children are baptized, they become full members of the church. No other action is necessary. Children need to do nothing more to earn a place in the community of faith and at the communion table. Baptism, of course, is a sign of something that has already happened; every person has been accepted as a child of God. But it's a sign, a symbol, that we parents can point to when we struggle to have our children included in the community of faith—to participate in both its cost and benefits.

Some people don't agree with this. They feel communion is an intellectual activity and that children aren't capable of understanding. But do adults fully understand? Do we also exclude mentally disabled or senile adults from the table? Can't they and children experience the mystical and spiritual as well as, and sometimes better than, adults? By excluding children, we buy into a hierarchical culture that values some people more than others. We accept the implication that one has to earn or deserve one's place.

Being different and being faithful at home

When parents make baptismal vows on behalf of their children, they declare that they will try to live a life that invites their children to follow the way of Jesus. The question is, how do we fulfill this commitment? How do we share the Christian story and the lifestyle it requires?

I got some clues about the story part from a film called *What Do You Think?* with Dr. David Elkind (Geneva Press, 1975). This film shows how children comprehend religious concepts at different ages and stages. Every time I see the film, I am impressed by an eight-year-old Jewish boy in it. He, more than the Christian children of the same age, knows the stories of his faith. I presume that he knows them better partly because the Jewish religion is not as commercialized as Christianity, so the Jewish stories and rituals don't get as mixed up with Santas and bunnies. But he also knows them because many of his religion's rituals were practiced, and the stories were told, in his home.

He would have learned about the Sabbath and its meaning each Friday night at sundown when family members made a point to gather for a meal, to light the Sabbath candle and to bless the bread and wine. Then everyone rested until sundown on Saturday.

Each fall, during Sukkoth (a Jewish harvest festival commemorating the temporary shelter of the Jews during their wandering in the wilderness) he would sense the brevity and insecurity of life as he and his family sat in a backyard hut, made of scraps from field and forest and decorated with the fruits of the harvest, and watched the stars or felt the rain.

At Hanukkah, in December, as he helped light a candle on each of the eight days of the holiday, he would hear of the victorious return of Judas Maccabee to the temple in Jerusalem, and of the one-day supply of oil that kept the Holy Light burning before the ark for eight amazing days.

At Purim, in February, he might act out the story of Esther, who saved the Jews from slaughter. And at Passover, as the youngest child, he would ask in Hebrew the four questions that explain why the family is gathered at a Seder meal—to remember their liberation as a people.

Christian children of the same age, in this film, knew that Santa brought presents at Christmas and that the Easter Bunny brought candy at Easter. That was what they had experienced in their homes. They may have heard some other things. But they learned most from what was *done*, not said.

Rituals for Christian homes

What can we do to make our Christian faith and story come alive for us and for our children? We aren't blessed with a set of rituals for the home as are our Jewish brothers and sisters.

In our family, we tried to develop some rituals of our own over the years. For Advent, we used to bring in a fallen bare tree branch to serve as a Jesse tree. Each evening, we hung a paper ornament on the tree. These ornaments symbolized Jesus' family tree, starting from the creation story up to the time of Mary and Joseph. Nancy and Bryan got so enthusiastic about this activity that they squabbled over who would look up and read the scripture passage referred to on the back of each ornament, and who got to hang David's shepherd's

crook or Moses' tablets. They learned a lot about the sweep
of history in scripture and of God's action in that ritual. But
as they got older, they felt this wasn't a "cool" thing to do. So
we got into the habit of just putting up the Jesse tree, with all
the ornaments already on it, early in Advent.

Sometimes we also put together a creche or manger scene,
piece by piece, throughout Advent, telling the story of each
item—shepherds, wise men, innkeeper and so on. Even now,
we maintain the tradition of lighting Advent candles each
Sunday in Advent. We have them in an Advent wreath in the
centre of our dining table. As we begin our meal together, we
remind ourselves of a world waiting in darkness for the light.

During Lent, we sometimes put different symbols of the
Easter story in the centre of our table each Sunday. Then we
discussed them—towel, pitcher, crown of thorns, whip, cross.
Or we lit candles set in a crown of thorns, remembering
Jesus' time in the wilderness, his ministry, and the price he
paid for announcing the arrival of God's kingdom of love.

I tried to say grace at suppertime every day—not as a
pietistic activity but as an act of gratitude for what we have in
life. But I didn't get very far. My children balked at this once
they reached adolescence. They would say "we don't want
any more of this God stuff. You bought the food and we
cooked it—not God." As a single parent with no other adult
to support me, I gave in and let the practice drop. Now I'm
amused when they expect me to say grace whenever we have
company or a large family celebration. They tolerantly
announce that "Mum always says grace at these occasions,"
and they frown when children who are not used to saying
grace giggle.

Living the Christian story

Doing things together helps us all reflect, learn, and recall
the Christian story. But we also need to experience the life
Christians are expected to live *because* of the story.

In our family, we visited the sick, the elderly, and the dying

together. When my mother was dying, we all shared in her
care and all stood by her bed, stroking her hair and saying
goodbye as she left this world. I did not try to protect my
children from sickness and death. I wanted them to know that
we are called to move toward such people in love and compassion, and not to back away in fear. God gives us the
strength and tenderness required in such situations.

We also participated together in peace walks and protests
to improve standards of child care in our province. We wrote
letters together to Christian brothers and sisters in jail in
Korea for their stands on human rights. We recycled our
garbage for the environment's sake. These, and many other
activities that we are hardly conscious of, helped us glimpse
the vision of God's community of love and mercy for all.

Children can learn about Christian disciplines just by being
part of our families and seeing what we do in the routines of
our lives—which may include daily prayer, meditation, Bible
study, and sharing our money, time, talents, and goods. We
can invite our children to participate too. Whether they choose
to or not, we continue to be a witness to them through our
daily practices.

Being faithful in the congregation

We parents have some control over how we organize our
home life so that all members can participate in and contribute to the family faith journey. In the congregation, the
situation is more complex—especially in congregations
where children are considered "different" from adults. Such
congregations need continuing reminders that they, the
baptizing community, baptize each child into full membership
of the church universal. Children need to be treated as valued
companions on the journey of faith who have gifts to
contribute *now* rather than in the future.

Congregations need to include children and all marginalized people into their communal life, not only for the sake of
the disabled, the illiterate, the senile, the people of different

races and classes, *and* children, but for their own sake. A
congregation demonstrates to the world what God's community is like. In God's community, the last will be first. All
people will have equal access to God's love. So to be a
community faithful to God's intentions, a congregation needs
to provide equal access for all its members. Including children.

Worship

Worship is the central activity of a community of faith.
Here, especially, it is important that all present, including
children, have an opportunity to open themselves and their
lives to God, to give thanks and to receive whatever comfort
or challenge or joy God has to offer.

Worship can't involve everyone every minute of the
service. But it can at least demonstrate the intention of including everyone. Even practical matters such as seating arrangements make a statement. Have you ever noticed who sits in
the very front rows (or the very back) of some congregations?
I have. I've been to churches where the front rows are taken
up by people in wheelchairs, or residents from nearby institu-
tions—such as homes for mentally disabled adults, psychia-
tric hospitals, reformatories. Often, the front rows are almost
reserved for children. Nearly always there are two or three
empty rows between them and the rest of the congregation.
What does such a seating arrangement say about God's community? No wonder hard-of-hearing adults don't want to sit at
the front; they don't want to join the ranks of the marginalized. They don't want to be considered like children—which
says volumes about how we include children!

Those who can't read or remember easily can usually join
in when there are repetitive prayers and responses in the
service. I remember as a child how pleased I was to be able to
sing "Holy, holy, holy" every Sunday like everyone else. I
could also say the Apostle's Creed and The Lord's Prayer.

People who are hard of hearing, or who can't sit still and

listen for a long time, need to *see* symbolic actions, such as lighting candles. They need to *participate* in movements, such as coming forward to take communion or giving an offering.

Representatives of the congregation need to share the leadership of worship, to show that *everyone* participates in God's ministry. I've seen people moved to tears as they watched a mentally disabled man who was thrilled to light an Advent candle. Children have brought scripture passages to life in new ways through drama and art. Lay people have sensitively addressed the worries and hurts and joys of the congregation in the prayers of the people.

As members of church boards or worship committees, or simply concerned parents and Christians, we can ensure that worship is planned to show that everyone matters—to God and to the community of faith—and that everyone has a ministry in God's world.

Sometimes people resist having children or some disabled people in worship, because their restlessness and unpredictability disturbs the quiet and dignity of worship. Parents need to remind others that congregational worship is not a *show* or a substitute for private devotions. Worship is a joyful, sometimes noisy, *gathering* of God's people.

Helping children to participate

My congregation worked hard to include children in worship, but the children continued to be inattentive and squirmy. I finally realized why. The children were so used to the service being irrelevant to them, and so in the habit of ignoring it, that they didn't even look to the front to see if anything new was happening.

Similarly, parents were so used to ignoring their children's inattentiveness and squirming that they weren't pointing out what was going on. I had a chat with the worship leader. After that, he began to say "Children, I want to be sure I have your attention. You are now going to see a dramatization of today's scripture. Watch this ox yoke and the whip." He explained each part of the service in a worshipful manner. The worship bulletin was numbered and illustrated so children could follow it. And parents were encouraged to help their children follow the service—even to help them read the hymns or count the verses.

The church also did a series of sessions on the parts of a worship service. Children planned and led the congregation in each part of worship—all the different prayers, presenting the word in scripture and sermon, communion, music, banners and symbols.

There was a remarkable change in the attentiveness of the children after this. But this process can't be a once-only affair. New parents and new children come along who need the same consciousness-raising about worship.

Education

The eight-year-old Jewish boy learned his people's story from doing things. Some were at home. Some were in his synagogue. We Christian parents need to make sure our children *do* things at church school to learn the Christian story—just as they do at home.

I've talked to hundreds of children in the church over many years. When I ask them what they wanted most at Sunday school, 99.9% of them said they wanted to do things, not to sit and listen. I know I would not be involved in the church myself or know the Christian story if I had only attended a Sunday school where we sat and listened as passive receivers of knowledge, or where we took turns reading haltingly from workbooks. I learned about the Christian story and life from mid-week groups. From a very early age, we took turns in these groups planning and leading our own worship. We did outreach projects for our church, our community, and our world. We acted out Bible stories, prepared foods mentioned in the Bible, talked about our own faith struggles, conducted meetings ourselves. We *did* things. We used our talents. We felt we had a ministry and a contribution to make.

Congregations need to offer exciting, active, involving educational programs that help children participate in ministering in God's world. Congregations need programs that help children know they are loved and valued even if they are "different." Parents can be the leaven or salt or light that moves the body of Christ in this direction.

Families can offer to read scripture or lead prayers or usher or take up the offering *together*. They can bring their children along and involve them when the congregation takes its turn at a local food bank. They can ask during a Board discussion on redecorating the Christian Education wing if the children have been consulted. They can suggest that the pastor visit or make a call on a child in hospital.

Decision-making bodies, mission

At home, we need to talk with our children as we journey in faith together, to care for them and let them care for us. Congregations need to do the same. We consult children at home about how to spend allowances, decorate bedrooms, or choose books and games. In the same way, decision-making committees in the church need to consult with children before making decisions that affect them, such as selecting a curriculum for the Sunday school.

These church committees need to remember that children are full members of the congregation. They have gifts to offer to the work of the church. Children can bring much joy as visitors to shut-ins. I remember when I used to take my toddlers to visit Mrs. MacIntosh, an elderly lady whom I had visited since my youth as part of a mid-week church program. Her eyes always widened with pleasure when she saw the children. She took great joy in introducing them to other residents where she lived.

Children also have needs that require care and attention. They too need pastoral visits when they are sick at home or in hospital. They need comforting and counseling as much as adults when there's a death in the family, a divorce, a crisis. I remember the feeling, as a little child, of being left out of the grieving and comforting process when my infant brother died. I couldn't put my feelings into words, so it was easy, I'm sure, for my distraught parents and family to think I didn't understand and didn't need comfort. But I did. Pastoral care visitors can play a crucial role for children in such situations. Often, those close to the children are hurting too much themselves to attend to them. A hug and a few words—"David, you must be missing your father very much"—can do a lot.

Children have great energy and enthusiasm to offer to projects where they feel they can contribute—from helping to clean up church grounds, to relating to a church-sponsored refugee family, to protesting pollution of God's creation. We need to ask them to *act* with us.

Involving children in the Christian story and the Christian life, at home and in the congregation, allows them to do and give and lead rather than just listen and learn and receive (important as this is). By *experiencing* the actions of the kingdom, children can better understand that they are an important part of the community of faith and that they can help care for God's world.

Even if our children later choose not to be outwardly "different" by being part of the church community, they will be inwardly "different." Their experiences will nourish and guide them.

CONCLUSION

Throughout this book, we've talked about being "in this world but not of it." When we parents raise our children to live according to Christian values, we put both them and ourselves in tension with our culture. We live in ways that our society does not reward. And so we need support to enable us to raise children who are confident of their self-worth and of their contribution to God's world, no matter how different they are.

We picked six areas where we had struggles living out our faith as we reared our children:

- living simply when society values people for what they have
- coping with the race to be the winner at all costs
- treating sexuality as a God-given gift
- facing up to conflict and loving our enemies

- trusting that God is with us in the crises
- being different by being involved in the church

We hope that as you read our parenting stories, you compared them to your own. And that in the "conversation" between ours and yours, you found encouragement.

Parents don't come wise. We often have children when we are fairly young (both of us did) and we often make mistakes. We try to be perfect, and we try too hard.

Children don't come wise either, although they often have wisdom for which parents don't give them credit. Parents and children both make mistakes, sometimes extremely bad ones. But Christianity—and the God we believe in—is about forgiveness, respect, grace, strength and love.

Because we try to love our children as God does, we must allow them the freedom to make their own life choices, as God does. They may not choose our values. But at least they will know what our values are. They will have seen those values in the way we live. They will have heard those values as we explained how the Judeo-Christian story influenced our behavior. They will have felt those values in the way we accepted and loved each of our children.

And we will know, whatever their choices, that we tried.

APPENDIX

Suggestions for personal reflection
or group discussion

by Carol Rose Ikler

Chapter One

1. Why is the story of Jesus and the rich young man (Mark 10:17–22) included in this chapter, which is about parenting young and teenage children?

2. Why is Jesus' message to the young man (Mark 10:21) difficult for many North American believers and families to apply personally today, according to the writer?

3. How does the story of the birthday party affect your feeling about your family ethics (or Christian beliefs about money) in your family of origin or your household now?

4. Some Christians feel that the real religion in North America, even for many avowed Christian believers, is consumerism, particularly that rooted in TV commercials and the "theology of the mall." How does the author support us as parents or family leaders in developing awareness and dealing with this problem?

5. In recalling her daughter's seventh birthday party, the writer remembers that "all the ponies looked at me with the round brown eyes of Ethiopian children, and the Cabbage Patch clothes were too tenderly made for a doll." What is the writer's basic concern?

6. Why is the writer critical of Barbie and Ken dolls? What is important about her observations?

7. Reflect on your present or past family experience in light of the following sentence: "The task then becomes one of negotiating between the values of the teen subculture and your own values as a family within the church."

8. What is meant by the phrase "vision of *Shalom*"? How does the writer connect it with Mark 10:17–22?

9. Think back over the exploration of parenting beliefs and practices in the entire chapter. Then consider how the following goal is developed: "We could begin by looking at what gives meaning to our lives: our theology." Note the emphases and headings (heavy type) within the chapter. How are they theological in content?

10. As an adult Christian responsible for the empowerment of younger Christians, what ideas or themes in Chapter One did you find personally challenging? Where did you agree or disagree with the writer's beliefs or practices? Which ones might be controversial for some readers?

Chapter Two

1. Coping with the race to be the winner at all costs is the subject of Chapter Two. Why do you agree or disagree that this issue is a major area of stress and challenge for a Christian family?

2. How do you feel about a parent's problem as expressed in the following sentence? "When I became a parent, I worried about how to help my children develop their abilities to their fullest … without making them feel like failures if they didn't win prizes or come first in competition with others."

3. How did the parent-teacher meetings at two different high schools give the writer "some insights into competition and the motivation behind it"?

4. What is your response to the writer's experience of seeing "children in tears at the end of the game"?

5. As families consider the prevalent notion "Winners are 'good,' losers are 'bad,'" what contrasting messages do they receive from society and the faith?

6. How did Jesus deal with competitive disciples? What point about God and our relationships is made when we remember that Jesus shocked those with power and status by associating with society's outcasts?

7. In the chapter section "So what do we do?" the author comments that because of her biblical reflections she had to try as a parent to live her vision of what God's world could be like, and then invite her children to join her. What is important in her vision? In what ways have you as a parent or family been able to live out some of your beliefs of what God's world *could* be like?

8. In discussing the following paragraph, reflect on the writer's conviction that there are "different points of view about athletic competition."

> We parents need to counter the atmosphere of high pressure competitiveness in our children's sports activities. Our bodies, minds and spirits are gifts from God, which we are to cherish and enjoy, not damage and punish in order to be better than someone else or to be a "winner."

9. The writer notes that "we should celebrate with our children when they do their best. But being best offers many temptations for Christians." What kind of temptations, in the writer's experience and in your own?

10. Because our culture often glorifies heavy competition, and sometimes violence, in sports and other areas of society, these values may spill over into the classroom, playground, and family. Hence, some elementary and secondary schools include cooperation and peer conflict management skills in their curriculum. What happens in the schools in your community? In light of your personal faith, your parenting approach, and the issues discussed in Chapter Two, what are your recommendations?

Chapter Three

1. From your earliest years to adulthood, who were the persons that significantly influenced you, positively or negatively, in your experiencing of and thinking about sexuality? In what ways?

2. Sort out and reflect on the ideas in the following comment from the book's introduction: "[I]t's hard to teach them tenderness when the idea of sexuality as a God-given gift is so different from what we see in our media."

3. Why do some parents find themselves "wounded and afraid" when their "adolescent children begin to discover themselves as desirable, physical, and independent persons"? Consider an underlying theme in Chapter Three: Some parents are disconcerted by their children's sexuality, partly because they as adults haven't gotten it all together about their own sexuality. Why do you agree or disagree? How are the questions of the children in the opening paragraphs useful in discussing the above topic?

4. Do you agree that the "choice in the bedroom at the party ... is going to have to be made by the majority of adolescents"? Why are self-esteem and adult sexuality on the part of parents seen as basic and ongoing factors in that decision? Share how you have nurtured self-esteem and provided parental modeling related to healthy sexuality, or describe what you experienced in your family of origin.

5. Underline or list the many important words, phrases and concepts in the Chapter Three section "What is healthy sexuality, anyway?" Identify the basic theological statements. In light of them, discuss your list. Where do you agree or disagree with the writer's ideas and theological interpretation?

6. In thinking about sexuality as a Christian, the writer uses the words *gift, dilemma,* and *promise.* In light of these words

(and any you would add), discuss the six suggestions in the section "Education about safe sex."

7. "If you love me, you'll do it" is a familiar teen refrain. Discuss the nature of this demand, including the fact that scripture is not clear about the "rules" but is very clear about God's attitude toward justice, love, and the goodness of sexuality. Discuss, too, the high vulnerability of teenagers in regard to the exploitation of one another's sexuality.

8. Ask volunteers to read aloud the parts in the two conversations between Sam and his mother (pp. 59–60); ask someone to comment on Rebecca's story. Then discuss: How is protecting children from sexual abuse significantly related to self-esteem, obedience, and one's belief about God?

9. In the section "Allowing children to question you ..." (p. 58) list and consider the most important ideas and sentences, such as "Children who are *not* heard are vulnerable." Discuss the tools suggested to help children deal with the possibility of exploitation and abuse. Include others that might be added.

10. In the section "And what if your child is gay?" discuss each of the main points in the "facts to ponder" paragraphs, pages 63–65. Why is it important for Christian parents to be familiar with this information?

11. Discuss the references to Jesus and the Gospels on pages 62 and 67. Why are they important for Christians to ponder in a responsible discussion about homosexuality?

12. The section "A note about sex roles," page 68, raises several significant issues related to parenting and justice in the family. Identify them, reflecting on their varying importance in the families of your church and community.

13. With which sections of the "creed" about sexuality and God, pages 68–69, do you agree or disagree? How do you deal with people who believe very differently?

Chapter Four

1. Our society frequently gives the impression that a family in conflict is not a success. What are some good reasons for Christian parents to question that notion? Discuss the ideas beginning with "Keeping up appearances vs. recognizing conflict" (pp. 72–76). Add your own ideas.

2. Reading and using the examples from the Gospels on p. 77, discuss the variety of ways Jesus dealt with conflict. Share how you have practiced or experienced some of his approaches in your family of origin or family now. What important ideas and skills in conflict management are illustrated in the story of Judy?

3. Examine and discuss the suggestions for dealing with conflict outlined on pages 78–81, beginning with "Acknowledge our differences." Which ones are more important? More difficult? What has been your experience as a child or adult in learning and applying the principles and skills included in these pages?

4. Using the "family case study" sections about Susan, Penny, and Helen on pages 81–86, the members of your group can volunteer to be narrators and to read the parts in the scenarios on pages 83 and 85. What feelings, principles, and skills connected with conflict resolution are indicated in these scenarios? Which of the feelings, principles, and skills can be found in most families?

5. Christian parents are called to enable children to apply publicly the conflict-resolving principles and skills learned at home. How do we help children to be "wise as serpents and gentle as doves"—to respond differently in different situations, as Jesus did? In light of the skills suggested earlier in this chapter, discuss the main principles outlined in "Applying learnings about conflict" (pp. 86–88). What would you add or omit?

6. The underlying theme in this chapter is that, since conflict is a natural part of life, the important response from parents is to *help* children "cope with conflict in healthy and creative ways that enhance life and bring peace with justice rather than destroy life and all creation." Discuss what is meant by the key words in this quotation. Illustrate in your own experience and in insights from this book.

7. In the beginning of the chapter, following a parenting story and comments, is this statement: "Christian parents today are challenged to think about how to raise children so that they can deal with conflict in ways that won't make them either 'Rambos' or back-stabbers." What are some of the alternative ways suggested in this chapter that you have found useful in your family?

Chapter Five

1. Discuss the kinds of crises illustrated on pages 89 and 90. What feelings do such crises evoke? Share and interpret one crisis from your childhood or your present family. As we parents respond to crises, why is our image of God so important?

2. Two major ingredients in responding faithfully to a child in crisis (pp. 91–94) are dealing with guilt and identifying the "deeper questions." How do the stories of Tracy (goldfish) and Cam (bike) point to these basic insights? Why is "listening at several levels" an important learned skill for parents?

3. The swim camp crisis encountered by Andy and his friend contained the potential ingredients for producing a lifelong emotional wound. What were the ingredients? What counter-acted them? Contrast society's "school of hard knocks" approach with the "intuitive respect and support" approach that evolved in the community around Andy.

4. Why is it important for parents to have asked the question "What is God like?" *before* a crisis demands it? Explore the six points on this topic (pp. 98 and 99) in light of the comments about Grandpa's death—"what is said and not said." What stereotypes about God would you discuss in responding to a family death crisis? How does your view of God reflect or differ from the six points?

5. Why are "crises with no rituals—like divorce" (p. 99) more difficult for families? How does your congregation or other churches that you have known respond to such crises?

6. Review the story of the teen party on page 101 following. What would you add or subtract from the process of *consequences*? Discuss the difference between consequences and punishment. How do your beliefs and practices regarding punishment or consequences relate to your personal image of God?

7. Read aloud and discuss the two stories of Jesus: the crisis of the disciples (p. 100) and that of Jairus (p. 104). How do these stories help you respond to the question "Where is God in our family crisis events?" Refer to the main ideas in the comments on resurrection (p. 106).

Chapter Six

1. Discuss the following two major points in Chapter Six, drawing on either your personal experience in your family of origin or your family faith journey in the present:
   • As families involved in a committed, intentional Christian lifestyle and a community of faith, we are set apart as "different" in today's society. How?
   • "Even if our children later choose not to be outwardly 'different' by being part of the church community, they will be inwardly 'different.' Their experiences will nourish and guide them." How?

2. As children seek their own identity apart from their parents, they must constantly sort through societal, peer and family values. Discuss in particular Bryan's search for meaning and models (pp. 107–109). What were the contrasting values from childhood to young adult years? Can you identify with any of Bryan's experience?

3. Recall the pervasive theme throughout this book: A parent's personal belief and practice about God profoundly affect the way the children are raised (pp. 6–8). Think about that as you review and discuss the challenging ideas on faith and action on pages 110–112, including:
- "… the lifestyle we are really called to live because of Christmas and Easter"
- "Many people today—young and old—recognize that the future of creation is in jeopardy…. Parents can offer their children an exciting opportunity—to discover God at work in the world, and to join with God in the task of healing creation."
- "Our children will serve God in their own way … but they will be affected."

4. How is the way of Jesus related to Christian baptism? Consider this question as you illustrate the ideas in the following sections (pp. 113–115), using your personal experiences in your family of origin and present family:
- "Being different and being faithful at home"
- "Rituals for Christian homes"
- "Living the Christian story"

5. Christians who take seriously Jesus' concern for marginalized persons (the poor, sick, disabled, women, children, outsiders, and so on) seek to follow his way in today's world (advocacy and justice) and in their congregations (affirmation, inclusivity). Chapter Six calls for the inclusion of children as a legitimate, intentional part of the community of faith, whereby parents and adult leaders seek to fulfill the

covenant of the sacrament of baptism. "Being faithful in the congregation" explores the areas in which congregations have an opportunity for developing and witnessing to a genuine commitment to inclusion of children in worship, education, participation, and mission. What was your own experience as a child? How inclusive of children is your church now? Add your personal illustrations to those in this chapter.

6. If you would like to put together your own set of review questions, refer to:

- The introduction, particularly pages 6–8, where the writers' goals and theological themes are introduced.
- The conclusion, pages 123–124, which points in brief outline to the major parenting areas and issues discussed in the six chapters.